JAN 16 2013

BON

The L. Ron Hubbard Series

BRIDGE PUBLICATIONS, INC.
5600 E. Olympic Blvd.
Commerce, California 90022 USA

ISBN 978-1-4031-9890-7

Special acknowledgment is made to the L. Ron Hubbard Library for permission to reproduce photographs from his personal collection. Additional credits: pp. 1, 9, 41, 75, 91, back cover Dman/Shutterstock.com; p. 11 AridOcean/Shutterstock.com; pp. 18, 25 Special Collections and University Archives, The Gelman Library, The George Washington University; pp. 30, 34, 36–37, 58, 61, 63, 66, 71 kanate/Shutterstock.com; pp. 72–73 Tetra Images/Getty Images; p. 82 Bruno Ferrari/Shutterstock.com.

Printed in the United States of America

The L. Ron Hubbard Series: Education, Literacy & Civilization—English

3 8001 00109 0145

The L. Ron Hubbard Series

HUMANITARIAN
EDUCATION, LITERACY & CIVILIZATION

Bridge

PUBLICATIONS, INC. ®

CONTENTS

An Introduction to
L. Ron Hubbard

"**I** HAVE BEEN ENGAGED IN A STUDY OF APPLICATIONS OF technology to illiteracy and illiterate or semiliterate populations and found some simple levels of approach." —L. Ron Hubbard

If seemingly a casual statement, it is not. That study of illiteracy spanned at least thirty-five years and culminated in a body of work that has factually changed the way in which we perceive the whole subject of learning; while as for those "simple levels of approach," we are, very truthfully, speaking of the answer to all that comprises a postindustrial educational crisis.

To those not yet familiar with the works of L. Ron Hubbard, let us begin with a few equally simple statements of fact: As the Founder of Dianetics and Scientology, he has received wide acclaim from many quarters; for drawing upon the central truths of those subjects, he has provided solutions to a wide range of critical problems. LRH drug rehabilitation methods, for example, are generally recognized as the singularly most successful and are now employed on six continents. Likewise, LRH methods for the rehabilitation of criminals are regularly applauded as the world's most effective and currently employed in penal systems across

Europe, the Americas, Africa, Asia, Australia and New Zealand. Then again, there is all the name L. Ron Hubbard means in terms of moral resurgence, a revitalization of the arts, sane and equitable administrative methods and, through Scientology itself, the realization of our most meaningful spiritual aspirations.

Yet when we speak of what L. Ron Hubbard has brought to the field of education, we are speaking of a very special commitment. For quite in addition to the founding of Dianetics and Scientology, he is also among the most widely read authors of all time, and it was with a love of words possessed only by our finest writers that he came to address the crisis of illiteracy.

"The inability to read," he noted in 1979, "is far, far more widespread and worse than anybody has imagined." Needless to say, he was right. Although given illiteracy trends through ensuing years, we have indeed come to imagine the worst.

Author, educator L. Ron Hubbard, England, 1959

To cite but a few telling statistics: notwithstanding this so-called information age, better than a billion people still remain illiterate and thus all but uninformed. Hence predictions of still greater gaps between have and have-not nations and commensurate political upheaval. Nor is the problem in any way limited to technologically impoverished regions. To wit: while some thirty million American adults cannot read an instructional manual, a good percentage of those lack the literacy skills for anything but the most menial labor. Hence predictions of a first-world leader with what amounts to a third-world workforce. Moreover, when weighing the cultural consequences of illiterate generations in the wings, we arrive at a chilling scenario wherein whole literary traditions are lost, precipitating what has been described as a new Dark Age.

One could cite much more. Illiteracy now exceeds 80 percent among juvenile offenders, prompting an Ethics Resource Center to conclude: "The fundamental tragedy of American education is not that we are turning out ignoramuses but that we are turning out savages." Then, too, of course, there is all that illiteracy costs in terms of lost productivity. United States estimates alone run into hundreds of billions of dollars. While accepting

UNESCO pronouncements on illiteracy as undermining transcultural understanding, the cost in human lives is incalculable.

schoolyard drug abuse, adolescent suicide and, ultimately, an erasure of even the will to learn. But for the moment, let us focus upon the most

"...decline in the quality of Western education is directly proportionate to the infusion of psychological and psychiatric methodology in the classroom."

So, yes, we have come to imagine the worst. We have also come to an era wherein illiteracy is no longer only an academic issue, it is a political issue and a heated one at that. It has further spawned a whole host of catchphrases, including: "the disadvantaged child," "the reading-impaired child" and the "no child left behind." Yet given we still ask, "Why can't Johnny read?" the debate continues over questions of teaching methods, testing methods and coping with failures therefrom. Whereupon we come to that most deceptive of all catchphrases: "psychological labeling." It is more than just another aspect of the problem. It is a cancer at the heart of the problem. In point of fact, the entirety of a fifty-year decline in the quality of Western education is directly proportionate to the infusion of psychological and psychiatric methodology in the classroom.

Far more can and will be said, including what psychiatry has engendered in terms of

visible consequence: the grim specter of the twenty-first-century student.

He is anywhere from six years old to about sixteen, at which point he has probably dropped out. He is not only North American, but also European, Asian and African—all lands factoring into United Nations' estimates that a good percentage of the worldwide population can barely read word one. Although not so easily measured, he is just as plainly taciturn, surly and dour. For whatever it's worth, his fashion statement is frequently criminal—literally inspired by prison-yard wear. Finally, and given appearances can be deceiving, there is also this to consider: having never read a book in his life, his intellectual range is roughly defined by video games, television shows, Hollywood films and the lyrics of pop songs. Accordingly, he can hardly express an original thought.

All of which brings us to an absolutely crucial statement regarding LRH tools for learning.

It is said that L. Ron Hubbard has been bold enough to assert that for any learning problem, there is a workable solution. Referenced herein are a few of several thousand educators who wholeheartedly agree. They hail from all continents and all scholastic arenas where they face that twenty-first-century student every day. Among other stories from their roll books are reports of once illiterate Los Angeles gangsters, now turned inveterate readers and once problematic inner-city students gaining two-plus years of reading proficiency after but a few weeks of instruction with LRH study tools. An introduction of the same into China's Shandong province led a worst-performing class to citywide honors, while the same again in Mexico City bettered passing rates on final examinations from 5 percent to 90 percent.

There is more. So salient were scholastic improvements across Southern Africa that entire school systems now employ L. Ron Hubbard's Study Technology. Yet the overriding point is simply this: when discussing Study Technology, we are not speaking of some new study aid, a memorization technique or phonetic reading program. Rather, we are speaking of a complete technology for study, the means by which any subject may be grasped. Nor are we discussing any arbitrary approach. On the contrary, these are the components of study—this is how we learn, and for all that has been touted in the name of education over the last hundred years (at least), this is wholly new.

Central to LRH Study Technology is a delineation of the three underlying barriers to study—never before recognized and yet constituting the sole reasons for all educational failures. That is, educators may glibly speak of Attention Deficit Disorders or Learning Disabilities, but it is claptrap. Their students are failing to learn because no one has ever taught them how to learn—how to identify the barriers to learning and how to overcome those barriers.

No less all-encompassing, and even more fundamental to the process of education, is the next great LRH contribution, the Hubbard Key to Life Course. It is aptly named and the title actually bears upon our last introductory point: if one truly comprehended what one read and heard and was likewise comprehended by others, then the whole of life would open. Such is the subject of the Key to Life—to strip away the reasons why one cannot comprehend and why, in turn, one cannot be comprehended. At the heart of the course lies a particularly egalitarian view of language, not as an obtuse subject for academic study, but a living, breathing vehicle for communication. To exactly that end,

Key to Life further reshapes English grammar away from a stultified body of rules to a real tool for meaningful expression. The result is a student who does not merely read and write as we generally conceive of it, but a student who is *empowered* with the language, adept with it and masterful. In fact, although technically a remedial program, Key to Life ultimately advances our concept of literacy to wholly new and startling plateaus.

"Our intent is not to just salvage a few students," L. Ron Hubbard declared. "Our intent is to reverse this whole decay." As we shall see, he was absolutely serious, and if the general decay of twenty-first-century education has latterly grown critical, the LRH solution

"Our intent is not to just salvage a few students. Our intent is to reverse this whole decay."

is all the more potent. In the pages to follow, we shall examine both the development of those solutions and their greater impact worldwide. We shall also, of course, examine L. Ron Hubbard himself as an educator and, by turns, the course of his greater journey to what has truthfully been described as a revolution in thought. ∎

Guam, 1927, where a sixteen-year-old L. Ron Hubbard embarked
on a long and extraordinary academic adventure

CHAPTER ONE

Education of an
EDUCATOR

Education of an
Educator

MONG OTHER ITEMS OF INTEREST IN A LATER SUMMARY of educational experience, L. Ron Hubbard would cite his very early examination of semantics, his instruction of Chamorro children on the island of Guam, his headlong collision with academic repression at George Washington University and his eventual return to that

institution for lectures on popular literature. He would further speak of training some fifteen thousand military personnel through the course of the Second World War, his training of many thousand more students of Dianetics and Scientology and, quite conservatively, his several hundred thousand hours of research into the process of learning as a whole. His obvious point: "It has been a long road."

In proper sequence, however, the story is this: As the son of a United States naval officer, Ron's early education was somewhat irregular. Between 1916 and 1929, for example, he had attended no less than ten separate schools, "and this one, in the fifth grade, had had long division (which I had not had yet) and that one in the sixth had had advanced multiplication (but no real long division yet) and so I was snarled

beyond belief by school." As the saving grace, however, his mother had previously attended a Nebraska teachers college and was otherwise amply qualified to serve as tutor. Then, too, he was an extraordinarily bright young man, reading at the age of three and a half and soon devouring shelves of classics, including much of Western philosophy, the pillars of English literature and, of note, the essays of Sigmund Freud.

In later lectures on the development of Dianetics, Ron would have much to say on psychoanalysis: his introduction to the subject (through one of Freud's own students, no less), his experimentation with psychoanalytic technique and his eventual dismissal of the theory whole cloth. There was, however, one aspect of the subject with particular relevance

An itinerant young scholar;
Tacoma, Washington, 1923

here: Freudian emphasis on word association. For the moment, Ron would only pose the question, "What could be wrong with a word?" In time, however, he would examine the matter from several angles and most especially from what he described as "the influence of a mislearned word on a life." Yet as regards his greater progress through the 1920s, the next significant milestone involved the teaching of those Chamorro children on the island of Guam.

The circumstances are not as unusual as one might imagine. Merely, having left the Hubbard family home in Helena, Montana, to join his father at the United States Navy Base at Guam, the sixteen-year-old Ron had taken what amounted to a midterm position as an English instructor of the native school. Classrooms were crude, textbooks outdated and his five- to ten-year-old students were more than occasionally unruly. An LRH diary entry from the island specifically tells of a student

Right
Guam, 1927: the sixteen-year-old L. Ron Hubbard as instructor of a Chamorro elementary school

knifing. The primary problem, however, was cultural and, by extension, political. That is, notwithstanding United States naval lip service and some reasonably sincere missionary work, the Guamanian student had been fairly poorly treated by his school system. In the main, he was held to be naturally dull and thus undeserving of any real concerted educational effort. Indeed, beyond rudimentary "letters and sums," the typical Chamorro could expect little more than "highlights of American history" to explain his place within an American domain, and periodic lectures on personal hygiene.

Students in L. Ron Hubbard's classroom, however—thatched and sultry though it was—enjoyed a very different curriculum. In particular, Ron seems to have stressed two significant points. First, he wished his students to appreciate the scope of the world beyond their shores and, second, he wanted them to understand how literacy held the key to participation in that world. As it happened, such a message would eventually prove highly objectionable to military authorities. But what is important here, actually very important, were Ron's methods.

He offers two examples. In order to convey the utterly foreign concept of a skyscraper, he tells of sketching nipa huts, one atop the other, until he had a sketch resembling the Woolworth Building. While to convey the equally foreign concept of a railroad train, he tells of hitching three or four ox carts together. If the point seems too simple or obvious, the underlying theory would prove vital and factually hits right at the heart of the learning process: how information is best assimilated and what accounts for the bored and exasperated student. Inevitably, LRH conclusions here would further explain the implicit problem in his closing anecdote from the South Pacific—why a young naval engineer would spend hours attempting to calculate the storage capacity of a gravel barge with advanced calculus, only to be informed by a native foreman, "You see those white paint marks on the front and back of the barge? Well, they tell you how much gravel is in the barge!"

In either case, however, it was the heart of American academia that held Ron's next

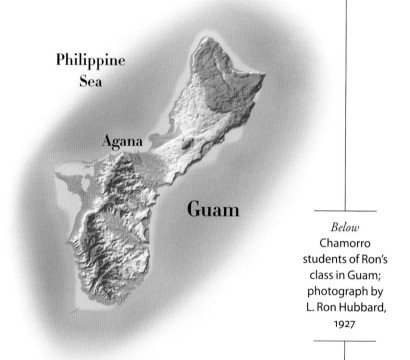

Philippine Sea

Agana

Guam

Below
Chamorro students of Ron's class in Guam; photograph by L. Ron Hubbard, 1927

lesson, and specifically George Washington University. He matriculated in the fall of 1930, after completing an interrupted high-school education in the space of about nine months. His declared major, at his father's insistence, was engineering. Although, in fact, he had already decided upon a literary career and was, besides, now very deeply immersed in research that would culminate in Dianetics and Scientology.

From the outset, George Washington University failed to impress him. He objected to instructors addressing students as "You!" or more formally, "Hey, you!" He objected to

a veritable "cult of mathematics" within the engineering department, and otherwise resented the emphasis on form as opposed to practicality. Moreover, as that first semester progressed and he drew a closer look—Ron would soon serve as president of his engineering fraternity—the view grew even bleaker. A "zero-zero world," he termed it in a later letter, and elsewhere spoke of a classmate expelled from the "saintly and sanctified" halls for publishing a campus newspaper article alleging university football stars to be illegal professionals (which was true). Eventually, however, and more to the point of the larger story, he came to focus upon the philosophic source of the problem, or what he would finally describe as the hidden curriculum within twentieth-century classrooms.

The issues are complex, and actually bear upon the whole shape of modern education as defined by educational psychologists John Dewey and Edward L. Thorndike. Ostensibly, their proposal was an advancement and involved a messianic view of the school not simply as a place of learning, but an institution for social adjustment.... Or as Thorndike himself so firmly put it, for "controlling human nature and changing it to the advantage of the commonweal." Central to the doctrine lay an equally messianic vision of society as a grandly ordered colony wherein each subordinates to the whole according to his talents. Those who would see parallels to communism, or national socialism for that matter, are correct. The roots are ultimately the same, i.e., German psychology and particularly Wilhelm Wundt of the Leipzig school. But in either case, it was a constrained view, literally a spiritless vision of the human being as the sum of his evolutionary parts. Thus, as Dewey maintained, if we are naturally social animals, it is simply because our evolutionary forebears naturally ran with the pack. While if, as Thorndike added, we also required molding to a civilized status, it is because we are not naturally civilized at all...and therein lay the rub, for suddenly and quite universally, the psychological shaping of a child was deemed far more important than the teaching of any traditional subject—be it reading, writing or arithmetic.

There is far more to this creed, of course, including a Thorndike proposal that children are best not even taught formal tools before the age of six, but rather educated only according to psychological priorities— which, in turn, opened the door to still more psychobabble on behavioral incentives, sensorimotor development and symbolic recognition. At the core of it all, however, lay an intriguing little model drawn from the behavioral school and specifically from the Wundtian offshoot of Pavlov.

Although never to embrace a single word of it, LRH offers as concise an explanation as any. One afternoon, on the trail of that extracurricular research to culminate in Dianetics, he entered the George Washington University psychology department, then headed by a Dr. Fred Moss (infamous among students for absurdly devious trick questions). There, Ron found the typical stock of white laboratory rats running a maze for bits of

Education of an Educator   13

cheese. When he inquired as to the point, he was provided with that classic behaviorist theory so thoroughly adopted by the Dewey-Thorndike school. (Dewey himself was among the first to conduct such experimentation.) That is, notwithstanding human intellectual capacity, we may still be defined in terms of the lower life forms from whence we evolved. Thus, just as the adolescent rat best runs its maze with the right combination of reward and punishment, so, too, does the adolescent human.... Except, of course, in human terms the maze becomes our educational system and rewards are generally less obvious than cheese pellets.

As we shall see, there is finally to be great irony here. For in attempting to adapt an adolescent to a psychologically acceptable norm—to the grand hive as it were—the psychologist would wind up with just the opposite: the sullen and illiterate killer bee who stalks today's schoolyard. But even as of 1930, that Dewey-Thorndike proposition carried disturbing implications; hence LRH objections to what he soon described as schools for "the pack," and students as "animated file cabinets." While even more to the heart of the matter: "It is appalling how education tries to reduce all children to the same level mentally."

His own stay at the university ended in the spring term of 1932, when the greater track of research toward Dianetics and Scientology drew him to ethnological work in the Caribbean. Yet the issues now at hand—that disturbing view of mass education to the needs of a massed society—he would never forget. Nor would he ever forget what psychology in the classroom represented in the way of declining literacy levels or what, in turn, he found when called back to George Washington University some four years later.

The circumstances require some explanation, but it is relevant to the larger story. Immediately upon his return from the Caribbean in 1933, Ron launched a literary career that would finally span five decades. He was not, however, to wait for success and, as of 1936, had firmly arrived at the forefront of popular fiction. The primary outlet for his work were the pulps—those massively successful pulpwood stock magazines eventually to launch the likes of Dashiell Hammett, Raymond Chandler and longtime LRH friend Robert Heinlein. In other words, when L. Ron Hubbard appeared before Professor Douglas Bement's short-story class at George Washington University, he stood for professional fiction. He stood for tales consumed by some thirty million readers and works that would forever live in American literature.

Opposite Douglas Bement's lectern, however, sat some fifty young men and women schooled in a very different view of American literature—or at least a different view of what it took to write the American novel. As a preliminary clue, Ron tells of discovering one of his own published works—on Bement's desk, no less—scrawled with such notes as "foreshadow" and "characterization." Also in evidence were various notations suggesting a pragmatic school of criticism and thus, by turns, yet another infusion of psychological thought.

Again, the subject is complex and bears upon a good part of twentieth-century American letters. But suffice it to say that quite in addition to the psychological novel as sprung from Freudian thought came a psychological infusion to the teaching of writing...and, at least in Douglas Bement's class, students who could criticize, but could not or would not actually write.

The point is not moot. Eventually through the course of his address, Ron would remark that a writer could not hope to develop a style in less than a hundred thousand words, i.e., a substantial novel or collection of stories. To a class of students bound for graduation after but ten or fifteen thousand words under their literary belts, the figure was shocking. A veritable uproar, Ron termed it, and cited actual complaints to the dean. But his argument was well taken, because George Washington University's creative writing department had not been turning out working writers. Nor, as he discovered through lectures in Massachusetts, had Harvard and, in fact, he could not name a single colleague from professional circles who counted himself a product of the university.

Below
George Washington University as it appeared when Ron matriculated in 1930

The "do-less graduate," he was eventually to term the ill-prepared collegians, and would soon make the subject a definite study. But for all intents and purposes, he was first to address a more pressing matter: the instruction of military personnel during the Second World War. The details were these: Following extended service in both the Atlantic and Pacific aboard antisubmarine vessels, Lieutenant L. Ron Hubbard reported to duty at the Naval Small Craft Training Center school in San Pedro, California. Duties were variable and involved both direct instruction of skippers and crews, as well as the redrafting of instructional materials for some fifteen thousand others. As one might imagine, the subjects were fairly technical: navigation, submarine defense and shallow-water assault. But in either case, LRH methods were entirely universal and actually spoke of very critical breakthroughs to come.

For example, in a preliminary note on his navigational text, he advised, "Concern yourself with the following definitions [e.g., *dead reckoning, latitude* and *chronometer*]. They must be well learned. Failure to learn definitions results in a later inability to understand explanations which include these definitions. Easily the most important factor in any study is a comprehension of what is meant by certain words."

Again, if the statement seems too simple or obvious, it is not. In the wake of the Dewey-Thorndike creed, and particularly through the latter 1940s, Western educators engaged in vigorous debate on such matters as the child's ability to distinguish ego from alter ego and the matching of curriculum to sexual development. By the early 1950s, education itself had become a highly obtuse term and was generally felt to best be described as "life adjustment." While even when the pendulum finally swung back to the more practical

curriculum of a cold-war science boom, the orientation still remained psychological (and, in fact, was largely instrumented by premier educational psychologist Jerome Bruner). In consequence came yet more convoluted debate on school as "life itself and not merely preparation for life," to quote Bruner himself, or school as a talent pool for a United States military-industrial complex. But regardless, as Ron repeatedly pointed out, no one had addressed that question of *how* one educated—beginning with such very fundamental matters as the comprehension of words.

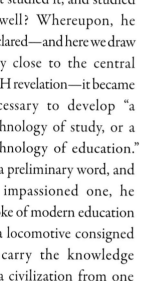

Thereafter, and particularly beyond 1950, when the founding of Dianetics necessitated training several thousand students on the subject, education remained a question of considerable LRH concern. For if nothing else, he asked, how could one practice Dianetics without having first studied it, and studied it well? Whereupon, he declared—and here we draw very close to the central LRH revelation—it became necessary to develop "a technology of study, or a technology of education." As a preliminary word, and an impassioned one, he spoke of modern education as a locomotive consigned to carry the knowledge of a civilization from one generation to the next. Unfortunately, however, those who had been driving that train had thrown the wrong switch.... And so, as he bluntly concluded, "the *Twentieth Century Limited* went off the rails." ■

Left
London, 1956:
It became necessary to develop a technology of study

"Dear Dean Wilbur"

Notwithstanding fundamental disagreements with the business of teaching at American universities, Ron would always acknowledge one notable "bright spot," William Allen Wilbur. Something of an institution as of 1931, whole generations of young men recalled Wilbur's slightly stooped figure in the former chapel where his freshman rhetoric class convened. The more appreciative among them further recalled his abiding love of Robert Browning and singular theories on Shakespeare; he seems to have regarded The Tempest as an encoded metaphysical dissertation. As referenced below, the wonderfully eccentric Dean Wilbur was additionally remembered for his perennial challenge that students compose a single sentence of three hundred words.... To which, Ron responded, "So I wrote a five-hundred-word sentence which merely said this: That a man was not permitted to think in the Western world and that this would inhibit any culture arising from universities. And when you go on that long with only one 'and' and one 'but' and no semicolons, it begins to build up a considerable velocity." It also landed the twenty-year-old LRH in considerable trouble and, in fact, he was finally informed "that unless I would write an entirely different theme expressing entirely different sentiments, I would be expelled from the university.... Proving my point!"

But he would not fault Dean Wilbur.

Dating from the spring of 1936, or when his rising star within popular American fiction returned him to George Washington University for lectures before Douglas Bement's short-story class, Ron's letter to the dean is as touching a tribute as any educator might wish. Also presented is the dean's equally touching reply, replete with his own subtle nod to the failings of regimented education. ■

March 16, 1936

Dean William Allen Wilbur
c/o GEORGE WASHINGTON UNIVERSITY
Washington, D.C.

Dear Dean Wilbur;

I was again at GWU for a few hours to talk to Douglas Bement's Short Story class. I had looked forward at that time to seeing you again, but I was informed that you had left the university—much to my disappointment and, I assure you, to the detriment of the school. However, I suppose you are enjoying your boats and a well deserved rest.

You could not possibly pick out my name from the tens of thousands of names which have passed over your class rolls. Perhaps you can best remember me for something I did which was rather worrying to you—a sad fact to be so remembered. I once handed you a theme at the term (probably 1931) which was one sentence, five hundred words long. On receipt of this you called out my name in class and asked me to see you afterwards. You were, I recall, rather shocked that anyone would quite dare hand you a critique of mass education under the guise of an English theme. It was, of course, rather bitter and, in a way, I have been rather sorry that I caused you concern. But although I apologized at the time I am afraid that the apology was more respect for you than disowning my ideas. And to complete the picture, I am tall and red-headed.

I hope that recalls me to you. It is noted only for that purpose. The real reason I am writing you is somewhat abstract. I have since done a little coaching on my own and I know that no contact is satisfactorily final unless you know that the man has either wrecked himself or made good, and it might be some small satisfaction for a master to know that his teachings have helped.

The engineering school was supposed to be my catapult to fame and fortune. My father had wanted me to be an engineer. My mother thought it was a sound profession, although both of them have, at one time and another, written and sold newspaper stories. I stuck to engineering for two years and college doors have closed no more upon me.

My profession, as I knew it would be from the first, is that of a writer. At present I am writing for the pulps—which is not a shameful or degrading thing as many people hint. I am giving the best that is in me for the purpose of entertainment and I find that many, many great writers first served their apprenticeship to blood and thunder. It is something to be a big frog in even a pulp paper puddle, to make excellent money, to be able to keep your own hours, and to shift whenever the scene grows monotonous, to be able to use a packing case in Nicaragua or a mahogany desk in New York at will. I am smugly satisfied that I have just started, and I am conceited enough to say that I write for the best of the pulps (ADVENTURE, DETECTIVE FICTION WEEKLY) as well as the worst.

When I wrote that theme for you (I wish I had it now) I was not referring to rhetoric, but to the rest of the university. Beside yourself, no other man there had anything to say other than dry, textbook things. That was not education to me. I wanted the contact of culture, perhaps, or maybe I wanted a chance to think. You were the only man there who would let a chap think. Walking into your classes or walking with you back to your office after a class was quite like stepping out of a hydraulic press into a spring day. You wanted a man to figure things out for himself and you respected your students. You were one bright spot in an otherwise zero-zero world.

This is not flattery, but something I have honestly wanted to tell you for some time. When I asked after you a year or so ago I was presented with a sight I shall not forget within my lifetime. I felt as though they had shown me something grisly when they pointed to the stack of books on Professor So-and-so's desk. They were nice, thick books, capable of breaking any student's arm. They were blue books and brown books and they contained the lot of them, thousands of stiff pages like starched collars—immensely respectable and utterly useless. These were the books, they told me, they were using *now*. These were the books which had taken the place of that stately little rhetoric manual—which somehow reminded me of a very scholarly little man with a taste for oddities, solemnity and vast kindness. I noticed they used book*s*, not a book.

Somehow—and I'm getting rather hard—I wanted to take off my hat as though I stood beside a coffin in which some close friend lay. Books, that's all they were. Just books. They were orderly and uniform and quite overbearing like pompous generals who bellow and rant and never say anything.

This all, of course, stamps me as a rebel, but I care nothing for rubber stamps. There was one remaining link between cultural and regimented education which had survived American mass production and that link was yourself. And now the chain is broken and the campus might as well hum with looms and lathes for all the individual personality it has with you gone.

Perhaps I should have been born an Englishman, in wanting something beside a Latin conjugation and a calculus formula from my school. Perhaps I expected more than I should have. Perhaps I had just grown up too soon. But I still wanted a university to be what it says in the name.

They told me, those other fellows (but you never did) that I was not doing my best, that I shirked and was lazy, that I had to get higher marks to match a machine-made intelligence test which made me out as brilliant merely because I had been over the world and back acquiring general knowledge since boyhood. They told me I would never amount to anything, that I was not a scholar. But you never did. You were quite willing to talk over all sorts of things and I appreciated it even though you have, most likely, forgotten.

Now, four years after leaving the place, I find that I was a scholar after all, that I am a student, that I have a keen and devouring interest for mathematics of all things, for history and economics and politics. I am studying because, for the first time in my life, I have been left alone. I have written several quality group (literary and artistic magazine) articles—which satisfy the mind but sadly not the stomach—on subjects for which credit hours are granted.

But I doubt in the extreme that I ever would have carried on had it not been for your very sane treatise on the world at large which you labeled "rhetoric" and which was nothing at all but culture, as alone and isolated upon a regimented horizon as a steamer's plume of smoke against the horizon.

I hope none of this makes you feel badly. It is not intended to be so. I felt all this long ago, but I was a student then. I am a professional writer now. I have earned a difficult thing, the permission to think and act for myself.

A year or more ago, I stood behind Douglas Bement's desk—so lately watching that same desk from the other side—and talked to his class about this profession of writing. The students were, many of them, attending when I was attending myself. I knew a lot of them by their first names. I talked to them about the profession of writing, not the art and I left them somewhat cold. No amount of impassioned argument could sway them aside from a foregone conclusion concerning the outside world. They were being taught—and Bement is a fair teacher—how to write they thought. That was enough. I was there, I told them, because Bement had delivered several erroneous remarks over the radio two days before on this profession of writing. I tried to assure them that out in the world they could sell their wares and save themselves from the ugliness of desks and time clocks, that they could make a decent living with a pen if they had it in them. Nobody ever told me that. I had to find it out through hard experience. But they did not want that worldliness. They wanted crammed facts. I did not talk to them with topic sentences and outlines, I talked to them because I knew what they would soon face. It was all for nothing. I could not shake them from a mental apathy which was quite as sticky as glue. They did not really want to think, and they would not even argue even when I spurred them to it.

I suppose this is what we call mass education. Frozen, fact-laden minds. Perhaps some of us should feel grateful for it because it is our own salvation. But I could not help but feel the sorrow of it. They were not being taught to think or study, they were being taught to gorge facts, however disrelated, obtuse or useless.

And out of all that vast shroud of darkness there had always been one sunburst, but it was gone. I went away from the university that night feeling melancholy. They had a pile of books sitting on a desk and they looked at them with pride and said, "Rhetoric? We've changed that. We have so many students (units such as 100 ccs. of water) to a class and so many classes to a professor and…." Squads right, column left and to hell with it, we've got too many to educate.

LRH as member of the George Washington University engineering fraternity, 1931; middle row, second from right

Your own definition of teachers will forever stand out in my mind as something beautiful and almost as rare as radium. It takes a genius to teach. You are that genius. From your rhetoric class, large as it was, there have come men I have since met, men who are thinking. No matter that those things fell upon so much barren ground. That could not be helped and never can be. There are many of us, casting about in this world, who remember and revere you. I have heard them speak.

Do not allow this to upset you in any way. Put it down that I am a rebel, a non-conformist, anything. Some of these days I am going to set down these things in a book, and your rhetoric, very battered now, will be open on the desk beside me when I write it.

At twenty-five it might be dangerous to think such things, it might be better to leave these matters to more regimented minds than mine.

However and whatever.... This letter was to be written to you this morning, hoping that you were well and telling you that you helped me in more ways than one....and here it is, some kind of a rabid essay on education and I'm certain you've had quite enough of that.

Anyway, here's the best in the world to the best man I ever met.

Best regards,
L. Ron Hubbard

THE GEORGE WASHINGTON UNIVERSITY
WASHINGTON, D. C.

331 Johnson Court. So.
St. Petersburg. Fla.

April 9, 1936

Mr. L. Ron Hubbard
40 King St., New York City

Dear Mr. Hubbard:

Your letter of March 16th was forwarded to me from the University and I thank you for it more than I am able to tell you. I have it before me now and I shall always cherish it. The realm of this fellowship is a deep realm of quietness and it does not often find expression. When it does it saves from loneliness and it stirs eternity in the heart. There is an exhortation of the Apostle Paul that fits this expression—"Study to be quiet."

I was retired from active service in the University at the Commencement in June, 1935, because of the age limit of seventy years. It came shockingly soon to me because the years had run on happily as though there were no limit. And associations with youth and the success of good English have no limitations. Then of a sudden a familiar phrase strains with finality—"as a tale that is told."

The University has been very generous to me, an honorary degree, professor emeritus, and historian to write the history of the University.

The fellowship of teaching is supreme in a teacher's life and I miss the experiences of this fellowship.

Thank you for all you write me about yourself beginning with the five hundred word sentence to your professional writing in the field of adventure and detective fiction. This is a field in which I have always looked for good reading and found it. You may think of me from now on looking for your stories.

I have been very happy in my friends and I shall love to count you among them, and to hope to meet you again. I appreciate what you say about my Rhetoric. When my health failed a year ago (I am in good health now) I had to leave all my work, and the men of the English department discontinued the use of the Rhetoric. It was my own theory and I had felt from the beginning that no one else would use it. But the actual experience of this was not easy for me. So you see your kindness means a lot to me—"a steamer's plume of smoke against the wide blue sky."

I am glad for what you write me about your professional career. I shall always think of you with affection and wish for you all that is best. My home will be in Washington and my address this University. I shall hope to meet you again.

Sincerely
Wm. A. Wilbur

Among other early LRH papers on schooling in the twentieth century comes *"Education."* It is drawn from a larger 1938 manuscript entitled *"Excalibur,"* wherein Ron first explored certain universal truths inherent to the later development of Dianetics and Scientology. *"Education"* reflects those same universal truths and does much to illuminate Ron's academic perspective.

EDUCATION

by L. Ron Hubbard

N O LONGER, IN OUR schools, do we have the rule of the rod insofar as I know. We do have a great deal of overwork in many of our schools as well as a great deal of useless baggage in the way of subjects.

But here and now let me say that a man who has had an unhappy schooling will never be able to find happiness unless he is capable of "arriving" at such eminence that it dizzies one to think about it.

It is appalling how education tries to reduce all children to the same level mentally. There are just as many degrees and kinds of intelligence as there are children.

The most heartless, useless, damnable thing ever invented was the group examination. It is here the class learns individual bitterness. The "bright boy" is not always bright. He has had a chance because he has security at home and his only fear in this life is that he will not become, perhaps, an engineer.

Such a boy is always infuriating. Such a girl is always just a little too smug.

Why?

Because on the examination paper, that boy or girl is shown to have more "intelligence" than the rest of the class.

"Society" is run for this boy and girl. Their mental equipment is average, their home life good. They have clothes just good enough and also looks just good enough.

Put to the real test, the boy and the girl are often found to be lacking in imagination but have what we call an excellent memory.

This is their main characteristic (and here we can almost generalize at that): they have complete confidence in their teacher. Their houses are well run and they are never hampered by a feeling of insecurity there.

The school puts its stamp on their diplomas and lo! The world takes it for granted that here is number-one boy and number-one girl and so it comes about that the boy gets a job.

He is told to go down to the dock and see how much gravel there is on a barge. Six hours later his boss comes down to see what is keeping him and lo! There is the boy sitting on a bitt, surrounded by sheets of paper, working his slide rule wildly, trying to arrive at the curve which will summate the gravel and...

It takes the boss five seconds. Scornfully he calls attention to the barge's draft and lo! The problem is solved.

This has so bewildered old-time engineers by its oft-repeated happening that a very unhealthy idea is current that "College guys is dumb!"

Naturally this boy was able to walk lightly through life on a very good brain and, too late, starts to use his stacked and uncorrelated memory files. When he sees a curve, he is deluged with formulas about curves and nothing else.

He has no imagination, they say. And this is right. He has had more facts than he has had problems—and those little things in the text are *not* problems.

Well, saith the professor with unction, then we have at last the perfect mind!

Not so. I am trying to say that a mountain of facts memorized is not education, never will be education and unless its practice is abandoned along with general examinations, we will continue to play havoc and will continue to drive our geniuses into the solitudes where they sometimes find happiness but where, more often, they blow out their brains.

This boy could have been made the equal of any high-ranking engineer or whatever on his graduation day simply by forgetting this foolish cram-cram-cram of facts, facts, facts without ever trying to correlate them.

How can that man's channels ever develop if all facts seem to be equal facts? Thus, when he thinks about a cow, ten texts on biology and six on industry and nine on animal husbandry instantly flood him and drown him.

And all the time, he merely wanted to know how to drive a cow.

Thus, the examination system is doubly bad. A man must memorize and swallow everything his books and teachers tell him without ever questioning any of it if he wishes to get a high mark. Let him question and he comes to half a dozen conclusions, one of which is an unhealthy one: the professor is a fool. But this is hard on professors because professors are not fools, but highly trained men held down by a system arising from the public hue and cry that Mama and Papa want to know what Johnny is doing in school.

That is up to the professor and up to Johnny.

The general attitude of students toward professors is really terrible to contemplate, much less hear. All the bitterness of the fellows who are really intelligent goes straight at the professor, who is, himself, only the victim of mass education.

A university professor must inherit all the errors. And a university professor deserves much better than that.

A worse system is at work than the university system, which in itself could be modified considerably if the basics become modified but which can do little until those basics *are* modified.

The YMCA schools over the country deserve much more credit than they get. They are small schools, true, but they are many. And young men have had their lives rehabilitated, not by any "Christianity," but by the type of teacher that seems to gravitate to these schools. They start a youngster down at the bottom and yank him to the top so swiftly that he never quite realizes that he has to study. And he knows more when he gets through a YMCA school, all the way through high school, than he would have known had he gone through grade, high school and college in any other place I know about.

There is a reason for this which is a very strange reason and does not seem, at first glance, to make good sense. In reality it has been considered a slap at these YMCA schools and has kept some of them from getting their credit ratings with any speed.

"In every man we place the sum of our own knowledge and thinking power."

He is not "taught" so much.

That is all.

He goes streaking through arithmetic to solid geometry with a lack of thoroughness which would grieve almost any educator. But when that boy comes out at the top, he looks back to a gleeful youth and, when he finally does come out, he knows more about the subjects than a man who has had to grind through twenty times as much data.

This is real education. We talk a lot about "education" and it, in itself, is so criminally general that I advocate junking it altogether and substituting "perception" in its place.

The Englishman gets a good chance to shake off his public school thoroughness at Oxford et al. because, strangely, he doesn't cover nearly as much, for instance, zoology, as his American brother.

We think the more facts we teach, the more the child will "learn." That is true—on an examination paper. But the child who cannot see security in facts will not parrot facts and so, that child is "dumb" when, in reality, he is the genius in the making.

This is the answer to that long-known riddle about the bright boy and the man who left college before he had scarcely started. The latter usually ends up bossing the former. If school is the end, it is only the end of happiness for the man who would parrot. All is bewilderment from then on and his mind is pitifully unequal to life.

There is an answer. And that answer must be applied unless we want to keep on educating and then shaking our heads in wonder over the educated.

The lad who stopped me one fine day and asked me what classes he ought to take knew that I didn't know any more about his future than he did. He's now in Luzon superintending a mine, but, strange to relate, he never studied mining anywhere. Only by completely leaving the field in which he studied was that man able to find happiness—and he studied gunnery at the Naval Academy and arts at college.

The greatest mathematical textbook ever written is about as big as the palm of the hand. S. P. Thompson, an Englishman, suffered so much in his calculus class that he gave to the world a priceless little gem called *Calculus Made Easy*. Any professor will tell you, just as Thompson said he would, that it is a "thoroughly bad book." Nevertheless, it zoomed many a boy through calculus who would otherwise have been maligned and made to feel defenseless through a flunk.

"We think the more facts we teach, the more the child will 'learn.' That is true—on an examination paper. But the child who cannot see security in facts will not parrot facts and so, that child is 'dumb' when, in reality, he is the genius in the making."

I am forever amazed at the inability of American students to speak Spanish. In Europe the children do not find it so difficult to speak three or four languages almost without flaw.

If we took four months to teach the first month's work of geometry, and then four more months to teach the second and third month's work in geometry, we would have students who knew geometry forever and a day—and it is forever and a day until death.

To criticize is not my purpose. I neither malign nor beg. To tell a professor that something should be done is to tell any man that he is not capable of doing right. But this must go by the boards as it has long obstructed this "progress" of which we are so fond.

The professor cannot help himself because he has a system handed to him by "precedent." Precedent, in itself, implies a lack of ability to think out a new course.

In every man we place the sum of our own knowledge and thinking power. This should be a law of some sort as it would solve innumerable ills in any line of endeavor. It should be written that a man should first discover the exact capabilities of his student or laborer and then work him accordingly. This should be the goal of industry, including the teaching of a superintendent to know the capacity of his men, or the factory owner to know the mental capacities of his superintendent.

We have forgotten this in our teachings and it is a thing which must be remembered.

Professors know so much they forget how little other people know. Thus, here is a working plan for better knowledge.

The baby sees something and looks at it wonderingly. Then it asks Mama what it is. She says it is a stove and it burns little girls. Three days later the baby is burned.

The baby listens to Mama telling her to say "Mama" and the baby merely coos. But Mama has some candy and says "Mama" and the baby cries "Mama" and thereafter thinks that Mama is a lovely word.

After the baby says, "Me ain't got some, Daddy,"

"Me too big enough, Daddy," and

"It was 'normous, Daddy," the baby begins to know English.

Am I right?

And then baby drifts along with "ain't" and "me" for "I" and with mispronunciations rampant until he is almost ten years old, at which time school begins to correct him very gently.

The baby grows up to five and begins to read fairy stories and goes around in the woods looking for a dryad to pop forth from a tree with a bag of gold which will never, never empty, no matter how one pours it.

These three cases should give some idea of a solution. In the first, it is impossible to *tell* anybody anything without enforcing it with fear or with example. The former case is the rule of the rod, but what a cruel, unnecessary thing! There is no reason to give pain to teach. There is no reason to say, "If you don't learn this, you'll never amount to anything." That is fear. It is also wrong to say, "You will be smart if you learn this."

Each one is fear of some sort and the last is a statement that the child is not smart.

If Mama had taken the little girl over to the stove very gently and had said, "See, there's a fire in it! Look how hot it is! It will keep you warm." The child thinks the fire pretty and admires it and, perhaps, starts to reach toward it. But it is *hot* close up. She withdraws with a foolish little grin and says, "Hot," and the trick is done.

In the teaching of language, the rule is invariably the same. One learns a conjugation and half a dozen words and then, suddenly, here is a volume printed in the language and off we go to the ponies and scribbled English over the words. What a waste of time for the professor and the student!

It is better to take another method entirely. First there are some very pretty romances about travel. South American countries, for instance, are among the most beautiful in the world. To the south of us we have a veritable paradise. And when we go there, we are fools as far as the language is concerned. Four years of Spanish in high school and college are not worth one month in Rio.

> *"As long as children and young men and women find pleasure in study, they will continue studying throughout life—and upon that depends their happiness."*

The bugbear of conjugation ought to be buried if we must learn languages. Correct conjugating is very pretty and accurate, but it is not worth a damn when one finds oneself on the beach trying to find the words to tell a storekeeper that he will sweep the place out for a meal. He usually thinks you are trying to buy a polo mallet.

I have tested it. A small American boy was once a friend of a Spanish boy and learned, in about a week, a hundred or more words in Spanish. Suddenly his mother took a notion the boy wanted to learn Spanish and sent him to a doctor who spoke Spanish well. Result? Complete wreckage of a future linguist simply because the doctor said, "Now this is *amar*. We say *amo, amas, ama....*"

Deadly ammunition with which to kill ambition.

Learning a vocabulary of five hundred words is not hard as long as one has no stumbling blocks which will convince one that speaking a foreign tongue is difficult.

I would like to see the result if some school taught such a vocabulary to its students with the statement, "This is Spanish. Nobody else in school except you students will know what you are talking about if you talk in Spanish."

Spanish motion pictures with the English caption on the foot of the screen and with plain dialogue will teach more Spanish in an hour than a text will in a year.

The class in history must not be made to parrot dates, for dates are nothing and easily forgotten. Rather, take periods in history and play upon the mind with a display of clothes, sports, children, kings, soldiers, politicians, sailors, boats, dogs, and, in short, the history of *people,* not events. Children are only interested in people, in children. That is all. A date is a date.

It takes brilliant imagination to be a teacher, it takes brilliant reasoning power to be happy in this world. If all children were taught to *reason* as they learned a few facts, they would have what nature intended them to have, a better castle for their defense.

As for other subjects, the less taught, the more can be correlated. For instance, in English, ask no child to say what Tennyson meant. No man in the world ever found out what Tennyson meant, much less Tennyson. But those stirring tales do what they were meant to do. The meter flows through one like music, and beautiful ladies and gay knights go dancing or charging through the lines. A brute like Lancelot is enough without wondering what Tennyson meant.

And there is English. And there is no surer way of driving children away from literature than revering that literature and making mumbo jumbo about how great it was. The worst of Dickens is in the *Tale of Two Cities*. Dickens really wrote some good stories such as *Barnaby Rudge*. That is enough to make anybody stand and cheer. But he turned it out like a true professional writer. He wrote to entertain when he wrote fiction and, by the wayside, he reformed the English school system.

It is not necessary to read one book by a whole class at once. That cuts down the zest. A child can give an oral book report if he is asked, "Did you like that story, Johnny?" "You bet. Gee whiz. That guy sure could fight!"

There are boys' magazines and girls' magazines designed for boys and girls which are enough to start a child upon a career of reading. The cinema has its points, but they are all lazy points in that they do not stimulate the mind to visualize. The movie hands it all out and leaves nothing to be rationalized.

And if we are to have bright children, we must teach them to *think*. Everybody has said that, but nobody had any real answer.

Many times men have said, "He never learned how to study," regarding some poor, bewildered fellow who did not have a "memory mind"—who had really learned how to study.

As long as children and young men and women find pleasure in study, they will continue studying throughout life—and upon that depends their happiness.

The ability to associate facts for the formation of a solution depends upon the facts possessed and upon nothing else. There is no knucklebone and tom-tom beating here. The human mind is clearly a tabulator and no man in an office is foolish enough to think that his adding machine will total his month's books until he has fed that machine the figures in the books. This is the unswerving law and is known well.

How then, may I ask, is it possible for anyone to solve anything until he at least has some small knowledge of it? How then is it that a trained thinker can take a few odds and ends of anything and arrive at a whole when men who have slaved in the field all their lives have not glimpsed truth? Such is the case of a young makeup artist, turned down by all the chemists in the country, who finally studied a few weeks and made his own plastic.

Everyone is baffled by this strange manifestation. But it is not strange and if we would let the children of Man lead happier lives, then we must teach them in such a way that any normal problem can be readily solved by them. To do this we must have facts. Real facts which will stay with the child.

To open the top of a cranium and into it empty forty books, to give the owner a diploma and a title, is not education but butchery.

We have libraries and need no animated file cabinets.

The boy and girl graduating at the top of the class usually, it is true, find some splendid position, but usually as walking file cabinets. This is not fair to them. True, their diplomas and rating did much to elevate them to high position because "society" appreciated such things. But the unhappy father is he who has a boy who suddenly grows tired and lackluster beneath the bombardment of facts,

"...if we would let the children of Man lead happier lives, then we must teach them in such a way that any normal problem can be readily solved by them. To do this we must have facts. Real facts which will stay with the child. To open the top of a cranium and into it empty forty books, to give the owner a diploma and a title, is not education but butchery."

the shame of failure and the contempt of elders. To this is generally added parental shame and even ire. Was there ever such madness?

At times a boy or girl with great reasoning power, and without great worry, rockets to the top of his class and holds honors and athletic achievement without seeming to be much concerned. Their lot is much better, *but* these are the real geniuses of the world and an educational system has prevented them from becoming the "successes" they might have been.

We face unemployment and many of the lesser tasks are being filled by men and women who were trained for better positions. The girl that majored in interior decoration can be found in a department store earning a ridiculous sum in contrast to what her education cost. The engineer turns surveyor because road-construction jobs are done by the nephews of the commissioners. The trained biologist finds himself, at forty, selling shoes.

This is not because they are less brilliant, but because there is an overstocking of the world in diplomas. In fact the men and women who have to take such positions are, like as not, the best equipped for the higher positions. It is a recommendation to graduate in the middle of the class—but not to the world of business. However, such things will very shortly be changed.

Any of these people make good educators, particularly when they have fought the world to their own great astonishment. If such people were to be placed in educating positions in their own line, the present overworked teaching staffs could have some small chance to live a calmer life without suffering financially or in reputation as, when the army expands, the sergeants always become captains. ✍

With the publication of Dianetics: The Modern Science of Mental Health *in May of 1950, and the many thousand readers soon requesting personal instruction in the techniques of Dianetics, L. Ron Hubbard returned to the matter of educating students in typically thorough fashion.*

As noted, his approach drew directly from Dianetics itself—from axioms relating to the way in which we maximally learn, our impediments to learning and, above all, teaching for application. In what amounted to a brief summation of his ideas, he presented the following instructional guidelines to the heads of Dianetics classes then springing up across the United States.

TEACHING

by L. RON HUBBARD

IF ONE WISHES A subject to be taught with maximal effectiveness, he should:

1 Present it in its most interesting form.

    a. Demonstrate its general use in life.
    b. Demonstrate its specific use to the student in life.

2 Present it in its simplest form (but not necessarily its most elementary).

    a. Gauge its terms to the understanding of the student.
    b. Use terms of greater complexity only as understanding progresses.

3 Teach it with minimal altitude (prestige).

    a. Do not assume importance merely because of a knowledge of the subject.
    b. Do not diminish the stature of the student or his own prestige because he does not know the subject.
    c. Stress that importance resides only in individual skill in *using* the subject and, as to the Instructor, assume prestige only by the *ability* to use it and by no artificial caste system.

4 Present each step of the subject in its most fundamental form with minimal material derived therefrom by the Instructor.

   a. Insist only upon definite knowledge of axioms and theories.
   b. Coax into action the student's mind to *derive* and *establish* all data which can be derived or established from the axioms or theories.
   c. *Apply* the derivations as *action* insofar as the class facilities permit, coordinating data with reality.

5 Stress the values of data.

   a. Inculcate the individual necessity to evaluate axioms and theories in relative importance to each other and to question the validity of every axiom or theory.
   b. Stress the necessity of individual evaluation of every datum in its relationship to other data.

6 Form patterns of computation in the individual with regard only to their usefulness.

7 Teach *where* data can be found or *how* it can be derived, not the recording of data.

8 Be prepared, as an Instructor, to learn from the students.

9 Treat subjects as variables of expanding use which may be altered at individual will. Teach the stability of knowledge as resident only in the student's ability to apply knowledge or alter what he knows for new application.

10 Stress the right of the individual to select only what he desires to know, to use any knowledge as he wishes, that he himself owns what he has learned.

CHAPTER TWO

Study
TECHNOLOGY

STUDY TAPES

RON HUBBARD

Study Technology

THE FUNDAMENTALS OF STUDY TECHNOLOGY WERE FIRST described in a series of 1964 lectures at the Scientology training academy of Saint Hill Manor in Sussex, England. As an introductory word, Ron spoke of how a sideline study of photography had provided an investigatory model. That is, by examining his own progress through a course of study, he was better able to isolate the barriers to study as a whole. Letters to instructors (he had enrolled on the famed New York Institute of Photography correspondence course) provide several concrete examples. For instance, having found himself somewhat "clouded up" on lessons relating to developing solutions, he eventually traced the problem to a typographical error—*contemporary* instead of *complementary*. Yet there is a far grander view of how he came to develop Study Technology and, succinctly put, it is this: If Scientology may be literally defined as "knowing how to know" in the most expansive sense of the word, then perforce it must contain the answers to how we acquire knowledge.

As another introductory word, he explained there had never existed a true technology of study. There had been a "technology of schooling," as he put it, including such incidentals as the shaping of curricula and planning of lessons. There had also been much on the theory of teaching on what educational psychologists have unashamedly described as the means of imposing ideas upon children. Yet study as the route to grasping ideas and mastering abilities—this had been neglected. In consequence, he spoke not only of educational decline, but also the decline of whole civilizations. Then again, he spoke of what had particularly befallen education since the Second World War and specifically the first indications of dropping literacy levels. Finally, and remembering we are speaking of essential truths drawn from the greater body of Scientology, he reiterated the universality

The First Barrier to Study

absence of mass or physical object one is studying

of Study Technology—which is once more to say: these *are* the barriers to study, and L. Ron Hubbard's solutions provide for the education of all students on all subjects.

He then proceeded with a discussion of those barriers and although his study methods comprise many principles and techniques, these are the fundamentals:

Absence of Mass

The first barrier to study he termed *absence of mass* and explained it in terms of a definite

physiological response to learning without the mass or physical object one is studying. That is, if one is attempting to grasp the function and operation of a tractor, the printed page and spoken word are no substitute for an actual tractor; and, in fact, lacking a tractor to associate with the word, or at least a picture of the machine, can inhibit all understanding. Among other adverse reactions stemming from an absence of mass, the student may, as Ron wrote, "wind up with a face that feels squashed, with headaches and with his stomach feeling funny. He's going to feel dizzy from time to time and very often his eyes are going to hurt." The student may further suffer boredom, exasperation and, significantly, a good deal more of what psychologists have tended to categorize as learning disorders necessitating psychostimulants. (While rather more enlightened educators have instinctively understood the principle as regards younger students, it has never received the importance it warrants at all levels of education.) But appreciating the principle in its purity, Ron explains, the solution is simple: supply the student with the thing itself or a reasonable substitute as in a drawing or photograph.

The Second Barrier to Study

too steep a study gradient

Too Steep a Study Gradient

The second barrier, he described as *too steep a study gradient,* and explained in terms of attempting to master a skill without having grasped a necessary previous step. By way of example, he offers the student driver unable to coordinate hands and feet to manually shift the gears of a moving vehicle. Although one would imagine the difficulty to lie with the act of shifting, in fact there is some earlier unmastered skill, perhaps simply keeping the vehicle on the road. In either case, the solution is simply a matter of cutting back, determining what the student had last understood and then isolating what earlier step had been neglected. Again, the reaction to skipping a gradient is both pronounced and physiological, and includes a confusion or "reelingness" that is frequently misidentified and so proves the ruin of many an otherwise-capable student.

The Third Barrier to Study

{ *all becomes distinctly blank beyond a word
not understood or wrongly understood* }

The Misunderstood Word

The third and most important barrier, he termed the *misunderstood word* and posed this question in partial explanation: have we ever read to the bottom of a page only to realize we cannot recall what we have just read? Therein lies the phenomena of the misunderstood word—all becomes distinctly blank beyond a word not understood or wrongly understood. Conversely, when the troublesome word is located and defined, all becomes magically clear. But in either case, one will invariably find a misunderstood or undefined word just *prior* to that "distinctly blank feeling, a washed-out feeling."

The matter is far more critical than one might immediately surmise, and of the three barriers, it is the misunderstood that most bears upon human relations, the mind and understanding. Indeed, it is the misunderstood word that establishes aptitude or lack of and, frankly, "it's what psychologists have been trying to test for years without recognizing what it was." It produces a vast panorama of mental effects and is the prime factor involved with stupidity. It also determines if one can actually *perform* a learned skill, and to what degree of proficiency.

In addition to the misunderstood word per se, L. Ron Hubbard further distinguishes the undefined or not-comprehended word. Nor, he points out with some emphasis, is the problematic word always obscure or highly technical. On the contrary, it is very often the simple article, preposition or conjunction a student fails to grasp, and that failure is both widespread and insidious. Indeed, batteries of subsequent tests revealed even university graduates incapable of defining such building blocks of the English language as *a, the, on* and *to*. While in consequence comes what Ron elsewhere describes as "little discomforts" with the language and thus inabilities to appreciate the shades of meaning embodied in words... which, sentence by sentence, paragraph by paragraph, can effectively lead one to misinterpret whole trains of thought.

The ramifications are actually immense, for in citing the misunderstood word, one is factually speaking of the root problem behind all inabilities. Without the misunderstood, one might or might not possess talent, but the capability to perform a skill would remain

> *"Precisely how the misunderstood word inhibits understanding, and thus ability, is a fascinating subject and bears upon both the essence of linguistics and the whole of the human learning process..."*

uninhibited. Conversely, a misunderstood in any field is followed by an inability to act in that field, which, as Ron further notes, explains the glib and seemingly bright student who graduates with honors but without demonstrable skills.

Precisely how the misunderstood word inhibits understanding, and thus ability, is a fascinating subject and bears upon both the essence of linguistics and the whole of the human learning process—how we comprehend words, how we translate words into ideas and how even a single misunderstood may derail an entire ideological flow. Integral to the matter is the LRH statement on grasping words conceptually, i.e., as symbolized concepts. Thus reading becomes not a matter of correctly pronouncing words, but gaining a clear and true understanding of the meaning embodied in those words. As we shall see, the misunderstood word further bears upon our perception of a subject, our affinity for it, and even our antipathy and aggression toward that which is not understood...as in—and this is no exaggeration—a differing race, culture or political system. Then, too, it is the misunderstood word that ultimately leads to an abandonment of a study and, lest the lesson be missed,

the 30 to 50 percent dropout rate plaguing so many American schools.

As we shall also see, students would eventually benefit from several LRH methods to locate and resolve the misunderstood word—Word Clearing, as he termed it—for it is literally "the subject and action of clearing away the ignorance, misunderstoods and false definitions of words and the barriers to their use." For the moment, however, let us review his broader treatments of Study Technology as contained in four pivotal LRH works.

The first is *The Basic Study Manual,* intended for any age or academic level beyond junior high, and offering a firm grounding in the detection and resolution of all three barriers to study. Next is L. Ron Hubbard's *Study Skills for Life,* offering the same fundamentals in an easily grasped format for the younger teenager, while the amply illustrated *Learning How to Learn* is expressly for the child. Finally, and for the definitive understanding of the subject, there is the Student Hat Course as taught in Scientology organizations. The term *hat,* incidentally, is drawn from Scientology slang and refers to the traditional notion of a hat as the badge of one's profession, e.g., a railroad engineer's cap. Hence the Student Hat provides what amounts to a professional grasp of LRH Study Technology and thus the skill with which to master any subject.

And the statement is not to be taken casually. As we have said, these barriers to study are neither arbitrary nor particular to the LRH methods. Rather—and once again—this *is* the subject of study, and the implementation of LRH solutions has proven nothing less than extraordinary. For example, in controlled tests of British schoolchildren, ages seven to thirteen, a mere ten hours of instruction in LRH methods proved equivalent to 1.3 years of reading gain. (While the control group, not

Drawn from some four decades of experience as an educator, L. Ron Hubbard's study methods represent the first comprehensive understanding of the actual barriers to effective learning. He developed a precise technology to overcome those barriers and thus how to learn and apply *any* body of knowledge.

The three definitive texts on the subject, *The Basic Study Manual*, *Study Skills for Life* and *Learning How to Learn*, essentially differ only in their treatment of the material; the first is designed for teenagers and above, while the second is aimed at younger readers, with the third offering the basics of Study Technology to children between the ages of eight and twelve.

He ensured that his educational breakthroughs were made available to young people in his *How to Use a Dictionary* picture book for children and his *Grammar & Communication* for children. And make no mistake about it, these works are making a difference—in the elementary school as well as in the executive suites of multinational corporations.

provided with the Study Technology, actually suffered a slight decline of reading levels, most probably owing to misunderstood words.) Not to be outdone are the Los Angeles students who, in the same ten hours of instruction, progressed 1.4 years in reading comprehension levels, and the so-called "disadvantaged" South African students, 91 percent of whom passed the rigorous national examinations with LRH Study Technology while 73 percent of their classmates failed for want of that technology.

One could cite much more, including those students with remarkably bettered IQ scores, instructors reporting significant improvements in classroom behavior and the once illiterate street gangs now devoted to the written word. Yet even considering bottom-line results, we are looking at something of enormous importance. For here is not another "study habits for success" or "tips for straight A's." Instead, here is the *anatomy* of education. Here is "bedrock on the subject of learning a subject," as L. Ron Hubbard himself described Study Technology and, very simply, it works. ∎

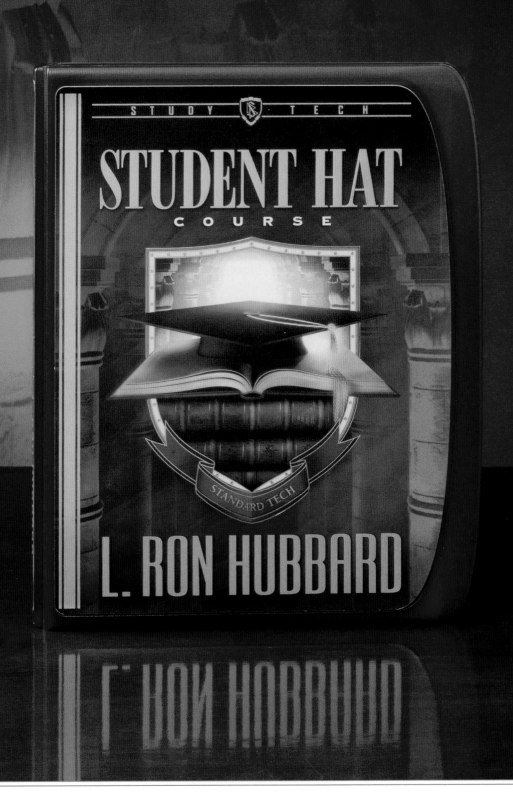

"*I have been using L. Ron Hubbard's study methods in Washington, DC, helping children to read. When the children come to my program, they are normally two to four grade levels behind. Some improved one and one-half to two grade levels during two hours a week attendance over a period of one year, whereas in the general school population no change occurs at all.*"
—William Tutman, PhD

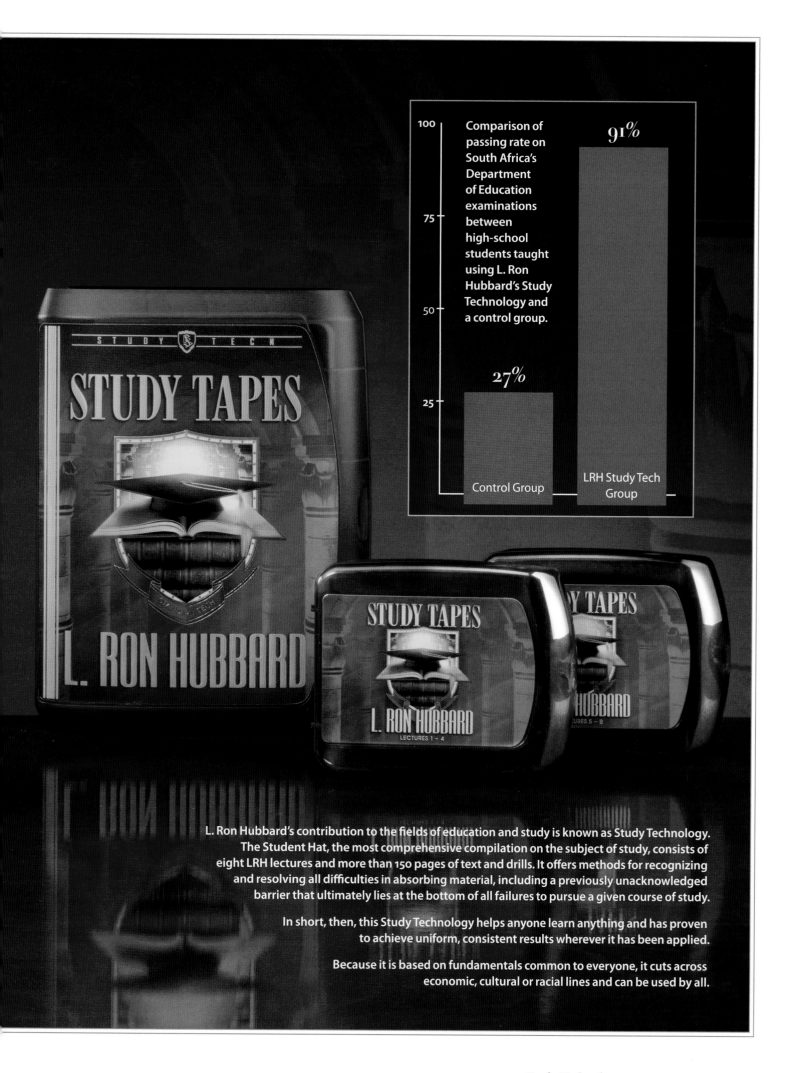

STUDY TAPES

S T U D Y · T E C H

L. RON HUBBARD

100

75

50

25

Comparison of passing rate on South Africa's Department of Education examinations between high-school students taught using L. Ron Hubbard's Study Technology and a control group.

91%

27%

Control Group

LRH Study Tech Group

STUDY TAPES
L. RON HUBBARD
LECTURES 1 – 4

Y TAPES
HUBBARD
TURES 5 – 8

L. Ron Hubbard's contribution to the fields of education and study is known as Study Technology. The Student Hat, the most comprehensive compilation on the subject of study, consists of eight LRH lectures and more than 150 pages of text and drills. It offers methods for recognizing and resolving all difficulties in absorbing material, including a previously unacknowledged barrier that ultimately lies at the bottom of all failures to pursue a given course of study.

In short, then, this Study Technology helps anyone learn anything and has proven to achieve uniform, consistent results wherever it has been applied.

Because it is based on fundamentals common to everyone, it cuts across economic, cultural or racial lines and can be used by all.

Word Clearing is an aspect of Study Technology defined as "the subject and action of clearing away the ignorance, misunderstoods and false definitions of words and the barriers to their use." As noted, a misunderstood word remains misunderstood until one clears its meaning to a point of full conceptual understanding. Given that the clearing of misunderstood words is so vital to comprehension, L. Ron Hubbard's 1978 delineation of the procedure is presented here in its entirety.

HOW TO CLEAR A MISUNDERSTOOD WORD

by L. RON HUBBARD

I**N RESEARCH CONCERNING** WORD CLEARING, study and training done with various groups over the recent past months, it has become all too obvious that a misunderstood word remains misunderstood and will later hang a person up unless he clears the meaning of the word in the context of the materials being read or studied *and also* clears it in all of its various uses in general communication.

When a word has several different definitions, one cannot limit his understanding of the word to one definition only and call the word "understood." One must be able to understand the word when, at a later date, it is used in a different way.

How to Clear a Word

To clear a word one looks it up in a good dictionary. Dictionaries recommended are *The Oxford English Dictionary* or the *Shorter Oxford Dictionary*.

The first step is to look rapidly over the definitions to find the one which applies to the context in which the word was misunderstood. One reads the definition and uses it in sentences until one has a clear concept of that meaning of the word. This could require ten or more sentences.

Then one clears each of the other definitions of that word, using each in sentences until one has a conceptual understanding of each definition.

The next thing to do is to clear the derivation—which is the explanation of where the word came from originally. This will help gain a basic understanding of the word.

Don't clear the technical or specialized definitions (math, biology, etc.) or obsolete (no longer used) or archaic (ancient and no longer in general use) definitions unless the word is being used that way in the context where it was misunderstood.

Most dictionaries give the idioms of a word. An idiom is a phrase or expression whose meaning cannot be understood from the ordinary meanings of the words. For example, *give in* is an English idiom meaning "yield." Quite a few words in English have idiomatic uses and these are usually given in a dictionary after the definitions of the word itself. These idioms have to be cleared.

One must also clear any other information given about the word, such as notes on its usage, synonyms, etc., so as to have a full understanding of the word.

If one encounters a misunderstood word or symbol in the definition of a word being cleared, one must clear it right away using this same procedure and then return to the definition one was clearing. (Dictionary symbols and abbreviations are usually given in the front of the dictionary.)

Example

You are reading the sentence "He used to clean chimneys for a living" and you're not sure what *chimneys* means.

You find it in the dictionary and look through the definitions for the one that applies. It says "A flue for the smoke or gases from a fire."

You're not sure what *flue* means so you look that up. It says "A channel or passage for smoke, air or gases of combustion." That fits and makes sense, so you use it in some sentences until you have a clear concept of it.

Flue, in this dictionary, has other definitions, each of which you would clear and use in sentences.

Look up the derivation of the word *flue.*

Now go back to *chimney.* The definition, "A flue for the smoke or gases from a fire," now makes sense, so you use it in sentences until you have a concept of it.

You then clear the other definitions. One dictionary has an obsolete definition and a geological definition. You would skip both of these, as they aren't in common usage.

Now clear up the derivation of the word. One finds in the derivation that it originally came from the Greek word *kaminos,* which means "furnace."

If the word had any synonym studies, usage notes or idioms, they would all be cleared too.

That would be the end of clearing *chimney.*

Context Unknown

If you don't know the context of the word, you should start with the first definition and clear *all* definitions, derivation, idioms, etc., as covered above.

"Word Chains"

If you find yourself spending a lot of time clearing words within definitions of words, you should get a simpler dictionary. A good dictionary will enable you to clear a word without having to look up a lot of other ones in the process.

Cleared Words

A CLEARED WORD IS ONE WHICH HAS BEEN CLEARED TO THE POINT OF FULL CONCEPTUAL UNDERSTANDING BY CLEARING EACH OF THE COMMON MEANINGS OF THAT WORD PLUS ANY TECHNICAL OR SPECIALIZED MEANINGS OF THAT WORD THAT PERTAIN TO THE SUBJECT BEING HANDLED.

That's what a cleared word is. It is a word that is understood.

The above is the way a word should be cleared.

When words are understood, communication can take place, and with communication any given subject can be understood.

While much scholarship has been devoted to the origin and function of words, as L. Ron Hubbard quite correctly points out, the ways in which words affect us have largely been ignored. That is the province of Word Clearing—how the misunderstood impacts upon learning and thus the quality of our lives, and how the problem is resolved. As noted, Word Clearing is part of the greater body of LRH Study Technology. Yet given the misunderstood can effectively block comprehension of whole subjects—mathematics, foreign languages, history—the clearing of troublesome words becomes enormously important. Moreover, it is the misunderstood that breeds individuation from a subject and, by turns, hostility. Hence the much talked about correlation between ignorance and crime, and hence those former Los Angeles gang members literally turning from weapons to books with the implementation of LRH study methods.

Finally, and bearing in mind how the misunderstood affects our command of language in general, there is all Word Clearing means as a tool for broad cultural revitalization. In the simplest terms, Ron speaks of the misunderstood word leaving us uncomfortable with words, inarticulate and taciturn—as in that grim specter of the dull and monosyllabic student. Yet even the seemingly erudite reader may suffer from what he described as small "misalignments" in comprehension and thus an inability to appreciate meanings conceptually—which is to say, one can read words as such, but cannot even begin to appreciate the breadth of meaning. As but one consequence, whole sectors of the population can no longer appreciate quality literature—underscored by the fact Charles Dickens was once read in every English public house to rapt and enthusiastic listeners, while the twenty-first-century bar offers wrestling matches on wide-screen television.

All this and more is the subject of L. Ron Hubbard's 1980 essay "Word Clearing: The Key to Communication, Education and Understanding." Although, as Ron himself once remarked, the miracle of Word Clearing must be experienced to be appreciated, he does much here to explain both the phenomena of the misunderstood and the stunning revelation that comes from clearing words.

WORD CLEARING: THE KEY TO COMMUNICATION, EDUCATION AND UNDERSTANDING

by L. Ron Hubbard

"Word Clearing" can be defined as the subject and action of clearing away the ignorance, misunderstoods and false definitions of words and the barriers to their use. (Word Clearing has no bearing on the diagnosis or treatment of any medical or psychiatric disorder, some of which include conditions of inability to use, arrange or remember words. Word Clearing applies only to normal students and public. Where mental or psychiatric conditions are encountered in some individuals, competent medical assistance should be sought.)

The relay of ideas from one mind to another mind or minds depends upon words, symbols, sounds, pictures, emotions and past associations.

Primary among these, in any developed culture, are *words*. These can be written or spoken.

While whole subjects exist concerning the development and meaning of words, all of them very learned and worthwhile, practically no work was ever done on the *effect* of words or the consequences of their misuse or noncomprehension. This is the sphere of Word Clearing.

What has not been studied previously or known is that the flow of ideas in any message or field of learning can be blocked in such a way as to suppress further understanding or comprehension from that point on. Further, the misunderstood word can even act in such a way as to bring about ignorance, apathy and even revolt. And it will definitely depress productivity.

Not only did these things remain undiscovered, but also, of course, no technology existed to remedy them.

The discoveries and their remedies comprise the subject called Word Clearing. It is part of a broader field known as Study Technology, but in itself Word Clearing has many uses and applications.

There has been a deterioration in scholarly literacy since the nineteenth century. This has been obscured by the fact that more people can read and write today than a hundred years ago. But an examination of what was read and written then compared to what is read and written now, even by scholars, shows a very steep decline. Compare the political speeches and literature of a hundred or even fifty years ago to those of today and the general decay of language will become evident. Even the common vocabulary appears to have shrunk.

Earlier, noticing that the public was more and more dependent upon radio, motion pictures and television, all of which contain the spoken word, I observed the possibility that these messages were not being fully received or understood by the public. Recently this was confirmed by a survey undertaken by an advertising association which found that from one-quarter to one-third of the television material of all kinds was misunderstood by the audience. The study was undertaken apparently to combat charges of misleading advertising. But it has other applications. It means, for instance, that one-quarter to one-third of these huge advertising expenditures are wasted. And it means more than that: these misunderstoods can easily generate antipathy and even aggression and a revolutionary attitude.

> *"The primary stumbling block to all these efforts—advertising, the military, general education and others—can actually be summed up as the misunderstood word."*

Part of this is caused by changing patterns of education. Today the stress on literature and the native language has lessened when compared to the rod and no-supper attitude of the nineteenth century.

Strangely enough, it is the military which often pioneers the increase of literacy in a culture. In World War I, the US Army is said to have found that 70 percent of their recruits could not read or write. Some of their efforts to remedy this survive today in the title of an intelligence test composed mainly of symbols which was called the "Army Alfa." The Egyptian Army, more recently, found their soldiers could not read nor write and became the spearhead of a campaign for Egyptian literacy. This is a technical age. Weapons and equipment are very technical and to keep them operating, soldiers must be able to read manuals. So an army is not interested so much in the quality of being able to read and write; it is interested in the quantity who can.

One need not stress contemporary school statistics—the protests of irate parents, the lowering of entrance and graduation standards, the decline of value of an education—as these are the continuing subject of headlines. A brave effort was made to increase the numbers of students and wipe out race and class distinctions, but unfortunately this was not paralleled by efforts to improve the quality of literacy.

The primary stumbling block to all these efforts—advertising, the military, general education and others—can actually be summed up as the misunderstood word.

Thousands of hours of research and hundreds of thousands of cases indicate this conclusion. And more than adequate evidence exists today that the developed techniques in Word Clearing handle it fully when properly known and applied.

When one speaks or writes, one has the responsibility of being understood.

On a narrow plane, there are ways to make certain one is understood.

On a broad plane, one also has the responsibility to see that tomorrow's public understands much better.

To oneself, one has the responsibility of understanding what he sees and hears.

And there is the bonus, using the techniques of Word Clearing, of recovering whole subjects and educations which were not understood at the time and subsequently could not be applied.

Wherever communication is being engaged in, given or received, the technology of Word Clearing will find beneficial use.

Origination

The originator of a message, it can be supposed, has some desire for his communication to be understood by those who see, read or hear it. Otherwise it ordinarily would be pointless to speak or write at all.

"The problem of being understood has a great deal to do with the literacy level of one's audience."

A century ago this was given more attention than it seems to be given today. Then there were subjects like "diction" and "elocution" which were considered part of the usual school program. Twenty-two hundred years ago, in Greece, these, with allied subjects, dominated the educational programs. Indeed, a person's reputation was largely evaluated on the basis of his ability to handle words. So it might seem that, regardless of developments, scientific marvels and expenditures, Mankind today is paying less attention to the clarity of his originations. Yet those originations are pouring out in floods never before equaled in history.

The problem of being understood has a great deal to do with the literacy level of one's audience.

Where mass communication is attempted, inevitably a certain percentage of the recipients will misunderstand a varying percentage of the message. But one need not apathetically accept this as the "way things are." One can campaign in general for a higher literacy level in coming years and generations. And there are many intermediate solutions contained in the messages themselves. It is quite possible to communicate even complex thoughts to relatively illiterate audiences.

On an individual mind-to-mind basis, it is relatively easy to communicate even when the other person is quite illiterate. There are old—and false—ideas that one is likely to "insult the intelligence" or offend someone by "talking down to him." The real error is to originate in such a way that one is *not* understood. One need not express pity or disdain for his "lack of education." And it has nothing to do with his intelligence. It has everything to do with the ability of the originator to communicate to that particular person.

Technology has been developed in Word Clearing to handle these points. It is not always possible to put this technology into effect in immediate situations, but some effort should be made to do so. And the technology should be understood. It was once believed that a primary cause of war between different nations was their language differences. In the interests of preventing "wars" or arguments with audiences and individuals, one should seek to minimize the potential misunderstandings.

Define Your Terms

In a technical and scientific age, there is a considerable growth of terminology. New phenomena and ideas are discovered which hitherto have had no labels. And so new words are introduced. This is true of every pursuit and advance in the society. But there are ways to handle even this.

"The originator of a message, it can
be supposed, has some desire for his
communication to be understood
by those who see, read or hear it.
Otherwise it ordinarily would be
pointless to speak or write at all."

Voltaire, the French philosopher, once said something to the effect that those who would argue with him should define their terms. He was on the border of a discovery. Arguments are most often prompted by misunderstood words.

If one found two people arguing, one might assume they were hung up in principles or desires or opinions. And, of course, this might be found to be the current case. But if one took each of these two combatants, one after the other, one would find, in their association or in their past, key words they used to each other that the other did not understand. While this might not always settle their differences of opinion, it would certainly take the flame out of their argument.

It is certain that their misunderstandings with each other had some footing in earlier misunderstood words.

Their error was in not spotting that they were using words the other did not understand or had wrong definitions for and then not defining those words.

This assertion might seem incredible until one has actually done the experiment. A husband and wife in continual combat on the subject of money. He continually uses the word "thrift" when discussing their domestic economy. We find in examining the words they use that she has "thrift" misdefined as "starving," whereas it derives from "thrive" and means "careful management of one's money and resources." Clarifying the misunderstood word at least brings about an alignment of intent. The husband never spotted that he had a word there which reacted violently.

The schoolboy aches to leave school, revolts, causes trouble and finally drops out. A careful review finds he actually went into despair over the brain-cracking terms of arithmetic many grades before. Coached and handled, he suddenly wonders whatever got into him and responds favorably. The originator of the arithmetic text omitted adequate simple definitions of the words. And even used far fancier words than was necessary.

There is a basic textbook on "Marketing" (the skills of placing goods and services in the marketplace and getting them known, bought and utilized) which bogs large numbers of its readers and is responsible for much noncomprehension of the subject. Seeking to trace why this was so, it was found in the very first paragraphs that it refused to define the word "marketing" and even said that it was anything you could make of it. The effect on the student was to not make anything of it! He would hang up in the first paragraphs of the book and fail to assimilate what is factually a very interesting and useful subject.

So hidden were these misunderstood words—as the person's reaction to them was a blank, if not an aversion—that the difficulties they caused went unnoticed.

In the field of education, a series of classes all in the same school were given intelligence tests and it was found that the further the child "progressed" in school, the lower his intelligence became. The children of eight, for instance, attained intelligence grades far, far better than the children of thirteen. All in the same school. The texts abounded in not-defined words. Such a circumstance could be avoided by a thorough and rigorous campaign to fully define words used.

To use a word, one should know its meaning or which of its many meanings one intends and then use it that way. Almost any civilized language has a very broad vocabulary available. Almost any nuance of meaning can be expressed.

Such people as the flatboat men of the Mississippi and rough and tumble cowboys of the Western United States, in the nineteenth century, developed a fad of using the most polysyllabic and improbable words in their utterances. They did it to impress, emphasize and overwhelm. Undoubtedly it had its uses, especially in quarrels. And it is to be noted that the principal pastime of the period was fighting. Violence of utterance cannot substitute for knowing what one is talking about.

Propagandists in the current century have developed a whole technique for redefining words so as to bend a population more toward their pattern of thinking. George Orwell's masterpiece *1984* contains some remarkable examples. Quite a few such examples can be found in modern school texts. "Liberty" becomes the "right to wear chains." Such a trend is a disreputable part of the natural evolution of language. For language evolves and language changes. Chaucer wrote poems in English around six hundred years ago and the language now is so different that one has to take a course in Chaucerian English to read them in the original. The plays of Shakespeare are currently drifting into average incomprehensibility due to the evolution of language in the last three and a half centuries. And for that matter, a modern soldier might have difficulty discussing military matters with a veteran of World War II. Words and terms change or the meaning may change while the word apparently is the same. "Whore" meant only "dear" in earlier times. Thus it behooves an originator of communications to keep himself studied, up-to-date and conversant with the common parlance. Otherwise what he intends to say might be received in quite some other way.

When one might believe that his meaning of a word can be mistaken, there are ways, useful in speaking and writing, of making certain that the meaning he intends is what is communicated. It is not good enough to simply assume that as all words are cloudy anyway, no one person can ever really understand what another person really means—although that argument was once advanced to excuse lack of definition.

If it seems to one that the word he is speaking or writing may not be understood, one can simply say it and define it right there and then. Such as: "Etymology—the study of the origin and development of words—is an academic subject." "His destination was the Hebrides—islands off the West Coast of Scotland." A blunt definition is almost mandatory when one announces the key word of his subject matter.

There is another method of defining in text which entails the use of synonyms. One follows a word with one or more synonyms for it. Such as "Her feline (catlike) features..." "His arms were like ebony—hard, heavy, dark and durable wood." "Do not indulge (pamper, humor) the child."

The trick is in doing it so as not to unduly interrupt the flow of prose.

Not to define at all is to be a speaker whose audience enjoys a good sleep or a writer whose works are not read or an individual who is often totally incomprehensible even to his friends and sometimes finds them argumentative and even quarrelsome. It is a matter of courtesy, not a matter of "talking down to people."

The originator of any message has the responsibility of defining the key and special words he uses and noting and more clearly defining when his words are not being understood.

"*Propagandists in the current century have developed a whole technique for redefining words so as to bend a population more toward their pattern of thinking. George Orwell's masterpiece 1984 contains some remarkable examples. Quite a few such examples can be found in modern school texts. 'Liberty' becomes the 'right to wear chains.'*"

There is a third method: write or speak only very simple language. O. Henry, an American short-story writer of the early twentieth century was reputed to have a masterful command of simple English words; and he was one of the most widely read and enormously popular writers of his day. However, he also used contemporary slang as well as specialized words of that period's criminal world and so his works did not last, as they became outdated. One has to differentiate between simple language and slang, for they are not the same thing.

Writing and speaking simple language is not without its pitfalls. Based on a very large number of studies, it can be said as fact that it is the common, smallest words of the language that are the most uniformly misunderstood! "To," "from," "as" and their like, to the number of half a hundred, are found to operate, in communication, as very thorough roadblocks. They go overlooked because they are so simple. Some polysyllabic word is such an obvious candidate for misunderstanding that it receives the concentration of attention; but "everybody knows" these simple words when they factually do not. A special sector of Word Clearing is devoted to clearing them up.

To express one's thoughts and emotions without the benefit of extensive vocabulary is difficult. A person with a small vocabulary of words is a sort of communication pauper. He often finds himself bankrupt in trying to say what he really means; and this can add difficulty to his life. An omission of expression dams up the normal flows of interpersonal relations. This even can become a fad in itself. As the working vocabularies of college students in the 1960s and '70s sank, they began to affect a hesitant and indefinite manner of speaking. Unfortunately such can be accompanied by a diffident regard for life itself; and it can result in a bewildered world where no one seems sure of anything.

One need not surrender all the majesty of thought and language. One need only be understandable. The modern politician has sought to look, speak and write like one of the "masses" he is seeking to reach; in doing this he unfortunately has sacrificed his imposingness and thus his command position. The task is to sound effective and even poetic while using very simple words. Abraham Lincoln, the great American president of the nineteenth century, who imposingly led the crusade and war to free the slaves, had this gift; a schoolchild today can easily read his speeches with a thrill.

In order to say something, one should have something to say.

To speak or write simply, the first step is to decide upon one's message. And the second step is to phrase it so that it communicates to the person or persons one is addressing with a minimum of potential misunderstanding of words.

Probably there are many as yet undeveloped methods and systems of clarifying what the words one is using mean. The Japanese have one: their writing is in Chinese characters, but in the upper right-hand corner they put small symbols which give the Japanese pronunciation. Japanese words are very homonymic, same sounds mean many things. When two Japanese find themselves in an argument over meaning, it is not uncommon for one to whip out a notebook and pen and draw the Chinese character for the other. The sound of the word did not define it, the full written character did. And so they resolve their definition differences. Possibly one could put an asterisk or other symbol after an unusual word and define it at the bottom of the page—it would certainly save many trips to a dictionary. Such systems are mainly lacking in English and European languages. But the development

"When one might believe that his meaning of a word can be mistaken, there are ways, useful in speaking and writing, of making certain that the meaning he intends is what is communicated."

and adaption of some would considerably ease the flow of communication by introducing exact definitions of the meaning meant. Such languages also suffer from being homonymic. Any lawyer can tell you that the courts are full of suits stemming from contract words that were not properly defined. Courts are a war of sorts and a dominant skill in a lawyer is phrasing; where this fails, suits can result. It all comes under the heading of the definition of words.

Words also have emotional associations, aside from cold dictionary meanings. The propagandist, ad copywriter, public relations man often have, or should have, a command of this aspect of words. But there is no dictionary devoted to the cataloging of such connections. They are in public use. They change, decade to decade. They have periods of being good and periods of being bad. Once "Fascist" was a commendable designation but is now a dirty word. "Profit" was once praiseworthy but has become questionable. In choosing words, one has to have some idea of their *current* emotional association as well as their pure definition. The understanding of one's hearer or reader is colored by the emotional association of some of the words one uses.

> *"...when you use a word which is unknown to your reader or listener or for which he has a misdefinition, anything that is said or written following that word will be, at best, blank."*

It is bountifully tested and proven that when you use a word which is unknown to your reader or listener or for which he has a misdefinition, anything that is said or written following that word will be, at best, blank. Therefore one should define or persuade definitions be done. It would be a mistake not to say what one is trying to say. The skill involved is stating what one means to state in the way one wants to state it and yet be certain that it is smoothly understood.

Thought is complex, but language is rich and in itself carries the largest burden of culture and enlightenment in any high-level civilization. It is there for use, not abandonment. The task is to reconcile the use with the potential comprehension. It can be done.

It is not enough to guess at definitions, for this too has the recoil of uncertainty. It is well worth mining in dictionaries and classics for their exact and sometimes numerous definitions. Words are not just a dry academic subject. They carry the tide of progressing civilization. They are for *use* in your livingness. They capsule the knowledge and content of the world.

The words used by an individual or a firm often form the main personality impression received by others. And when they are not understood, then the individual or firm is not understood.

Pronunciation

The spoken word can be easily understood only when it is properly pronounced.

Mispronunciation can occur through ignorance, local dialect or accent. Dictionaries go to great pains to give pronunciations and should be given attention. They cannot, however, entirely represent the effects of localities on language in general. Some people pride themselves on being able to ascertain exactly where a person is from by listening to his accent.

There are more than forty-seven distinctly different accents in England, even though it is a small country. There remain a great many different accents in the United States. The inhabitants of Paris continue disdainful of all the different accents of French spoken in the "provinces."

Radio, then the motion pictures and now television, have served as great levelers of accents. Before radio it was nearly impossible for a person from Kansas to understand an inhabitant of Maine and vice versa. Local dialect even went down to the level of cities and, as in New York and London, districts of cities. Accents were *thick*.

In traveling about extensively, one had to rapidly master the local dialect wherever he went or be thoroughly out of communication. Not only was he identified as an outlander, he simply couldn't get his message across. He might as well have been talking the language of the South Sea Islands. The English, then intolerant of "colonials," had a solution for it. They talked much louder. Bostonians had a solution. They didn't deign to talk at all. It hardly ever occurred to anyone to learn just to talk in that dialect. He would have been understood and he would have comprehended; but this was dismissed as "artificial" or "posing" or "mocking."

"It is not enough to guess at definitions, for this too has the recoil of uncertainty. It is well worth mining in dictionaries and classics for their exact and sometimes numerous definitions."

There is a skill in mastering a dialect. In addition to learning their most-used words and the variations of meaning they give them, it is relatively simple to duplicate an accent. One studies where in the body and head they originate their speech from and then does the same thing. The upper part of the mouth, the nose, the throat, the chest or stomach and many other parts of the upper body can, any one or two of them, serve as a point of origin for speech. Just find the point or points from which they are speaking and speak from there yourself and you will have the basis of their accent.

With the broadening use of radio, local dialects began to soften and merge toward a national accent. The motion pictures began to talk and avid audiences of children began to imitate the accents of their heroes and heroines. And accents again moved away from individual districts toward a national tongue. And then when television appeared, the younger generation was plopped down in front of it to get them out of mother's way and the different dialects began to die out to be replaced by more national pronunciation.

So what is, then, the "national accent"? Factually it is what the actors and announcers say it is. Probably it is the language of the stage. This language has its own peculiarities: it is designed to reach out across audiences with minimum voice strain and maximum enunciation. Audience comprehension takes precedence even over character representation.

One can then predict what will become even more firmly established as the accent and pronunciation of the language of any nation or countries associated by common language: it will be that accent and pronunciation used by the most-heard radio, motion picture and television personalities. Once it might have been what university one attended, but this too is bowing to the dominance of radio, motion pictures and particularly television.

If one wanted to assume or use the most comprehensible accent and pronunciation, he would look for it in the contemporary average of the spoken words of announcers, actors and actresses which pour along the channels of public entertainment. This would be true in any civilized language today. Imitation rather than education is the route this seems to have followed in the last half century. It is a responsibility these people have never really assumed, but it is one that they fulfill.

"To speak or write simply, the first step is to decide upon one's message. And the second step is to phrase it so that it communicates to the person or persons one is addressing with a minimum of potential misunderstanding of words."

Spelling

Around the time of Shakespeare, the great playwright and poet of about 1600 A.D., it is said that writers prided themselves on new ways to spell things. This may be true, but in the last four centuries things have certainly steadied down. Spelling is remarkably standardized.

In English there are still some differences in spelling between England and America: "labour" in England is "labor" in the United States.

From time to time someone tries to introduce a new way to spell a word, mostly by shortening it. In America in the early part of the twentieth century, even the president was attempting to get "thorough" spelled "thoro." But today's dictionary lists it as "a clipped form of thorough."

Spelling seldom changes.

Incorrect spelling can introduce a misunderstood word into one's written communications.

One has some responsibility of spelling what he means if he wishes to be comprehended.

The current dictionaries have the last word on the subject of spelling.

The typographical error in print is an inadvertent misspelling and it too can introduce a misunderstood in print. It will have the same effects on the reader as any other misunderstood word. The answer for the writer is to proofread where he has a chance. It is mainly the responsibility of the publisher. The answer for the reader is to query where he cannot make it out and to demand errata sheets for texts where typographical errors occur. Even punctuation can throw a misunderstood into a text where it is incorrect or omitted.

Legibility

In handwriting, illegible words can introduce misunderstoods in one's letters, manuscripts, notes or copy.

When the typewriter moved into the scene, handwriting began to move out. As evidenced by specimens of the handwriting of students, it is no longer given much attention in many schools.

Unworkable systems of training in handwriting began to appear about the same time as the typewriter. The systems made handwriting very slow and students, in an effort to speed up, began to violate them and went into a no-system and illegibility.

The notes of meetings of around 1850, taken down during the meeting by the appointed secretary, are something at which to marvel. They are often in "copperplate," which is a style of writing you only see today on the fanciest wedding invitations. They are beautiful, like a work of art. Yet they were written at full speed, curls, ornaments and all.

At the end of the nineteenth century, reporters, not yet having typewriters, could write legible script as fast as a man could talk.

These skills can be acquired. Possibly even the systems that taught them could be dug up and put back into use.

If one wants one's handwritten communications to be understood, he should be careful of legibility. The minimum system would be to look over what one has written and where words are not easy to read, print them above the written word.

There is quite a bit in the subject of handwriting. People get an impression of personality from it and some experts even claim to be able to read character from it. Parents often form their opinion of the quality of his school by how well their child has learned to write by hand.

Handwriting is a bit of a lost subject and should be revived. One doesn't always have a typewriter to hand. Illegibility can introduce a great deal of misunderstanding.

Volume

Anyone seeking to verbally communicate to others, whether in their presence or over a telephone or via tape or radio, motion pictures or television, should have a good command of the subject of volume.

Hardly anyone does. Yet it is often the key to getting one's words understood.

The principle is to be just loud enough to be clearly understood. Too low, one's syllables cannot be made out. Too loud, the discomfort of receipt shuts off the willingness to hear.

The hearing of a person can be trained. Even when there is nothing wrong with their ears, few people have any sensitivity to the quality of sound. It is a trained response. A professional sound mixing engineer, who adjusts the sound quality and volume of programs, becomes painfully aware of this general inability when he seeks to train someone to help him with his work. It is a great oddity: as an audience, the average person's reaction to sound is quite sensitive; when one tries to train him to regulate the sound on programs, he begins in a complete muddle. The point is that many people cannot judge what they are listening to, whether good quality or bad quality, too low volume or too high volume, but nearly *all* people *react* acutely to defects in heard or recorded sound.

A well-recorded program, playing with good quality at the correct high and low sound levels, will get an audience response of "great orchestra" or "fine program." A badly recorded program with incorrect high and low volume settings will get an audience response of "terrible group."

Thus we have a sort of odd general condition. People know when the recording they hear is bad, yet they cannot tell one *why* it is bad.

The first observation of this occurred in the 1950s with a group of students. They were listening to a taped lecture and more than half of them were drowsy or totally asleep and the other half was inattentive. This could have been caused by many things: the heat of the room, the time of the day, the lecture material and so on and so on.

One of the possibilities was the recording quality of the tape player and its speaker system. So, as one test, a decent set of equipment was assembled and a tape of the same series was played to the same students in the same room at the same time of the day. The volume was correctly set. Success! The students, unaware they were part of an experiment, were bright, alert and cheering.

Much more study of this attention phenomena was undertaken. It was found that good quality and correct volume permitted the students to understand the *words* easily. Poor quality and incorrectly set volume, too loud or too low, either one, marred the ability of the students to understand the words. And it was this inability to receive individual words in the lecture at a volume and quality level they could tolerate that was putting them to sleep.

The moral that was learned was correct volume. Not too high, not too low, in any part of a program compared to any other part. The sound engineer calls this "dynamic range," meaning the range in volume between the high points and the low points of a program.

Errors are continually committed with this in motion-picture recording and mixing. This is currently because the type of tape they use will take a dynamic range that is very narrow. (For the expert, it is actually minus 9 to 0 on a recording volume meter.) Above and below that point, the sound distorts. Also, the type of speakers used distort the sound when it is too low or is too high.

In television, they often increase the volume of the commercials. If one adjusts the set to the commercials, then the program comes over too low in volume. And if one adjusts to the program, then the commercials come over too loud. Contemporary television sets have very small and very poor speakers in them and they will not take a wide dynamic range.

"The main reason for audience reaction is: they can understand the words or they can't."

There are actually not too many good sound engineers in the world despite the dominance of electronics in this age. Part of this is a lack of any real textbook on the subject and part of it is that, to date, electronic equipment used in this field is generally poor, unreliable and requires a superexpert technician to set it up and a genius sound engineer to operate it. What passes in the "industry" (as they refer to the motion-picture world) for "quality" sound is on the average far below what even a hi-fi buff (an amateur who tries to get everything he can out of his recording equipment in any way he can) would consider acceptable. This is one of those "well-known facts" about the "industry." The top makers of their equipment shrug when challenged and say, "Well, they don't demand any more than what we give them."

Yet, by the various studies of audience reactions, it is sound quality and correct, narrow dynamic range between highs and lows which make a program acceptable. The audience doesn't know why, it just "knows."

The main reason for audience reaction is: they can understand the words or they can't.

So if someone responsible for the audience acceptance of his program wants to make certain it will be given attention, he must, among other things, give attention to recording quality and volume. Otherwise they won't understand some of the words and it will turn them off and they will turn the program or stay away.

Good sound can be recorded, mixed and broadcast even with contemporary equipment. It does, however, take a lot of care and trouble and expertise. It tends to be a somewhat neglected area at management level. But it *can* be done.

What, one may ask, does all this technical discussion have to do with one's own ability to be understood and be heard by his own hearers in the same room? Volume has a very great deal to do with it.

You have seen people crane forward to make out what another was saying. You have seen them lean back when someone was speaking too loudly.

There is also another factor: the ability of the ear to adjust to volume or even whether or not it does. The eye adjusts to light that is too bright or too dim. But it takes a while for it to do so. There may or may not be similar studies about the ear—if they exist, they are not very widely known.

When one first steps into traffic, the sound sometimes seems appalling, but after a bit it seems "normal." A forest seems deathly quiet as one enters it, but after a while one can make out all manner of noises—of leaves and insects and birds. This is explained commonly with "getting used to it." The possibility is that it takes the ear—or the person himself—a few moments to adjust to changed overall sound volumes.

So there may be another factor in just speaking or listening to someone nearby. Dynamic range—the difference between the highest and lowest sound volume—may apply as well.

If one said the first syllable of a word loudly and the second syllable very softly, it is unlikely that that word would be understood. It would end up as a misunderstood word in speech.

But however that may be, in order to be comprehended, one must adjust the volume of one's voice to the distance the person is away from one, to the capability of his hearing and, sometimes, to the echo reflections of the room or the absence of echoes. And having established that volume, one should not change it *too* much within words and phrases.

Actually it is quite a skill and it is not paid very much attention. Yet violations of it may make the speaker seem incomprehensible. Misjudged volume, when too low, may lose whole words or even the whole utterance; when too loud, words and even the whole utterance can be closed out.

Volume also has a personality aspect: people who speak too softly are considered retiring or shy; and people who speak too loudly are considered overbearing or arrogant.

Usually people count on others to regulate their voice volume for them: too soft sometimes gets a "What did you say?" and too loud sometimes gets an "I heard you!" But with some practice one does not need these regulators.

The first big step forward on volume is to recognize that it exists and the next step is to learn to control it.

Good volume control of one's voice is often associated with "cultured."

At the bottom of it all is simply whether one's words are heard and understood. The reactions and effects when they are not can be quite surprising. And when they are it sometimes paves the way to a smoother life.

"Words are not just a dry academic subject. They carry the tide of progressing civilization."

CHAPTER THREE

The
KEY TO LIFE

The
Key to Life

"THE POSSIBILITY IS THAT WE HAVE A WHOLE CIVILIZATION which is out of communication." —L. Ron Hubbard

So epidemic is the failure to grasp written and spoken communication within this culture, concludes an LRH note circa 1980, "one should not ask further why it is failing." In particular, he cited those statistical links between illiteracy and violence, illiteracy and economic waste and illiteracy as a factor in political unrest. He also now spoke of functional illiteracy or hidden illiteracy as a serious impairment to living itself, while even the most articulate among us are stranded in a "world out of communication."

At issue here is the subject of the Key to Life Course: why we cannot understand one another and what that failure means to this culture as a whole. How this course came to be is a simple enough matter. In 1978, while working with students who had passed through American and European public schools in the 1950s and 1960s, Ron noted literacy levels far below any he had previously encountered, short of Berber tribesmen in Morocco. In the worst, but by no means isolated, cases "they can't read English in any shape or form and in their common lives are reading stop signs as advertisements to the disco." Even former university students were found deficient and unable to comprehend the potboilers read for amusement. (Thus the telltale LRH note regarding a student who lost his grip on a western adventure after having read "mounted his roan" for "roamed around the mountains.") Moreover, the deficiency was ingrained so that students had eventually come to believe—and this again from a telling LRH note—"Isn't that the way everybody reads?"

Subsequent research told more. Fifty percent of the American population could not read an eighth-grade text. The attendant American dropout rate was five times that of Japan, and a full fourteen times that of Russia. The annual cost of such a crisis to United States industry ran into the billions; hence a United States Department of Labor warning of "devastating consequences" owing to illiteracy within the American workforce. Meanwhile, a random selection of thirty American schoolteachers found not one able to fully comprehend standard classroom texts (including a thirty-first tested, who had actually authored sections of the text). Finally, and here we come to the core of the problem, still another LRH study revealed reading and communication skills to be substantially lower than even students themselves had imagined. That is—and this point is crucial—one might presume he reads and communicates with clarity when, in fact, he does not. Hence that altogether chilling LRH conclusion, "The possibility is that we have a whole civilization which is out of communication."

LRH notes on the causes return us directly to that Dewey-Thorndike proposition. In a blunt word, he wrote, the modern schoolroom is a psychological factory for social reform and has nothing whatsoever to do with education. Curricula tends toward "eradicating faults instead of in the direction of acquiring skills," while testing encourages memorization "instead of use of the data to think." In the same sinking boat are instructors convinced their students are incapable of learning and, actually, encouraged to dismiss the problem as "Disorder

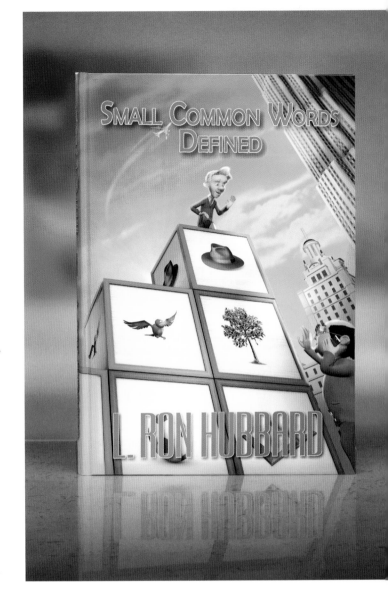

of Written Expression" or "Reading Disorder 315." Whereupon the psychiatrist steps in with any of a dozen psychotropics, and the child is now not only "Educationally Dysfunctional," but may suffer headaches, insomnia, abdominal pain and that so-called "major complication" from withdrawal—suicide.

There is more, including television and video games—not only obliterating the printed page, but effectively hypnotizing whole generations—and both psychiatric and illicit drug use to the same dead ends. Next comes what psychology has wrought as the dominant postindustrial creed, including a view of the child as something to be molded, while his teacher stands armed to the teeth with tools derived from

These materials comprise the Hubbard Key to Life Course, which breaks through the barriers to comprehension and assimilation of data, utilizing thousands of pictures to communicate the fundamental factors of language. It produces a person who is literate and who can express himself easily and clearly, both verbally and in writing, and who can fully understand the communication he receives from others.

animal experimentation. Finally, and bearing in mind all that ensues from the misunderstood word, there are the typical textbooks themselves with one undefined term after another to further stultify, bewilder and confuse.

Thus Ron developed the Key to Life Course—to methodically strip away impediments to comprehension and provide the tools for communication. As a first critical step, he speaks of resolving an especially baffling "chicken-and-egg" question, i.e.: how does one convey the meaning of a word to students who do not understand the words used to teach them? For a sense of the problem, consider opening a standard English dictionary to the first entry. The linguist may be satisfied, but the

average reader is not, particularly as he ponders unexplained phonetic codes, derivation symbols and the like. Worse still, even the simpler children's dictionaries can hardly avoid complex terminology. Consequently, the question remained: how does one convey the language—its construction, words and usage—without exposing students to yet more misunderstood words?

The LRH solution was the illustration, or actually thousands of illustrations, enabling students to grasp what they might not understand with merely the written word. For example, students are initially taught the procedure of Word Clearing with illustrations only—illustrations of readers referring to

"I always did well in school. I graduated from the University of California with a good grade average. I could memorize and regurgitate facts and data and even rearrange the data and express it in terms of exams and essays. I was considered very bright by my teachers and friends.

"What nobody knew was that I actually understood very little of this data—about 5 percent or 10 percent. I have changed due to the Key to Life Course. I totally understand the material I am reading. I am not memorizing. I am not filing away. I actually KNOW it. The Key to Life Course has rehabilitated my ability to learn." —T.M.

A sampling of the more than two thousand illustrations in L. Ron Hubbard's *Small Common Words Defined,* the only dictionary to visually convey all working definitions of those words forming the foundation of the English language

dictionaries, selecting appropriate definitions and more. In the same way, students are provided with the foundation of an English vocabulary, the means to use a dictionary and the essentials of English grammar—in precisely that order and all through illustrations.

A look at the actual LRH texts will further explain. There are three LRH texts central to the Key to Life Course, although not necessarily exclusive to that course. Indeed, much of what comprises the Key to Life Course was originally designed to stand quite on its own in any educational arena—the public school, the adult remedial class and even the most basic literacy program. The first is appropriately entitled *Small Common Words Defined.* It offers the sixty most commonly used English words, the building blocks of the language as it were, and thus those words absolutely necessary to define all others. As noted above, definitions for those sixty words are conveyed through illustrations. That is, words are defined not only with words, but also with illustrations. The device is quite revolutionary, for whereas every children's dictionary is amply illustrated for better comprehension, the illustrations are not actually integral to the definitions. With L. Ron Hubbard's *Small Common Words Defined,* illustrations are not only integral, they *provide* the definitions. The result is a student who grasps those building blocks of English regardless of literacy level, and with those building blocks then firmly in hand, he is ready to take up the next vital LRH tool, *How to Use a Dictionary Picture Book.*

How to Use a Dictionary Picture Book likewise teaches through pictures and so reflects the fact one cannot open a standard dictionary, even those for young children, without encountering terminology and derivation symbols neither generally understood nor adequately explained (a problem, incidentally, the modern curriculum has utterly ignored). In either case, the student does not possess the wherewithal to clear a misunderstood word. To precisely that end, *How to Use a Dictionary Picture Book* offers concise explanations of phonetic codes, punctuation, abbreviations and more. In this way, it provides both the tool for comprehension and the ultimate means to a powerful vocabulary.

The third and most talked-about text in this series is L. Ron Hubbard's *The New Grammar.* It logically follows from the previous texts; for with his grip of English building blocks and use of a dictionary, the student is now prepared to learn the way in which we best communicate.

"The Key to Life Course has opened a new life for me. I read something and I get it, immediately, or I find the word or symbol I need to clear up to get it. I have the potential to understand and apply anything I may be interested in." —U.V.

HOW TO USE A
DICTIONARY
PICTURE
BOOK

L. RON HUBBARD

you need to use a dictionary.

There are many kinds of dictionaries.

Some dictionaries are very big.

There is a dictionary which contains so much information that it needs many, many books to hold it all.

Chapter One
**What is a Dictionary
Dictionaries**

Dictionaries are different and they may define word

Most dictionaries are similar though, and when you learn to use

dictionary you will be able to use other dictionaries

The utterly unique L. Ron Hubbard's *How to Use a Dictionary Picture Book*
provides the missing link within all elementary education—the understanding
of terminology, symbols and nomenclature of the English dictionary

Introduction to The New Grammar

By David Rodier, PhD, Associate Professor of Philosophy of Language, American University, Washington, DC

English is now the language of international communication. It is the language used by heads of state. It is the language of international business negotiation. It is the language of the majority of the rapidly growing masses of computerized information.

Unfortunately, most persons educated by the public education systems in the United States are not competent in understanding and using English. As a teacher in one of the better private universities in the United States, I am well aware that many of our students, even though they are among those ranking very high on standardized tests, are unable to read with comprehension. Failing to master the full resources of the English language, students become functionally illiterate.

This inability to fully understand and use language causes problems in schools and businesses, and these problems affect wider areas of society. In this time of widespread illiteracy, L. Ron Hubbard introduces a book that makes grammar understandable and useful to all.

This book takes grammar and makes it easy. It helps individuals to understand the basic building blocks of the English language and how to use those building blocks to better communicate, express their thoughts and understand what they read.

L. Ron Hubbard first gained fame as a writer at a time when even the popular magazines of the day expected their readers to appreciate breadth of vocabulary and variety of style.

Only a professional writer with a writer's sensitivity to language could have written such an innovative approach to grammar. Only such a writer would see grammar not as full of constricting rules, but full of possibilities for rich expressions of thought and action.

Teaching writers how to write in the 1940s, L. Ron Hubbard has now come full circle with this grammar book and returned to the field of teaching language.

This is a brilliant book by a brilliant mind. In fact, it is a revolution in thought. ∎

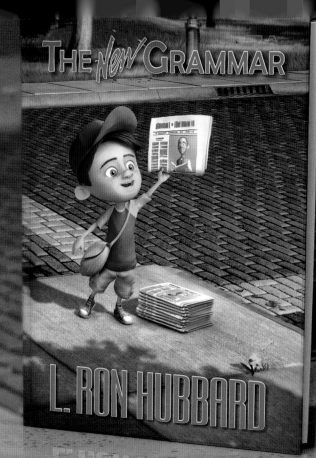

THE *New* GRAMMAR

L. RON HUBBARD

"I have gained myself on the Key to Life Course and an ability to duplicate others and to be duplicated by others. I feel like a new person who has shed tons of confusions and fears and who has tools to enable me to live life." —T.P.

"Thoroughly confused and stultified by the educational system, I somehow stumbled through life this far. It took the Key to Life Course to undo years of incorrect training and education and put a foundation there that will stand for the rest of my life." —F.A.

chosen. A flying bat's ...ound. So now when ...is object.

Bat

However, there are other things which can also be represented by the same sound. For example, when a ball is hit by a bat it could be thought to make the sound "bat." So this same sound, and its written symbol, is also used for an entirely different thing or idea.

Bat

Then the same sound or symbol which is used to represent the object—i.e., "BAT" as in baseball bat—can be used to represent the action done with or by that object and so we get the same sound or symbol being used with a different meaning. The action is not the same as the object even though they are related. In the following example, you see a ballplayer bat the ball.

Bat

Chapter Four
The Basics
of Language

A revolutionary treatment of the subject, *The New Grammar* is the first complete and yet still comprehensible explanation of the way in which we use the English language

The Key to Life   83

A revolutionary work, *The New Grammar* embodies a thoroughly practical view of the language with grammar as "the way words are organized into speech and writings so as to

> *"The possibility is that we have a whole civilization which is out of communication."*

convey exact thoughts, ideas and meanings amongst people." In that regard, grammar becomes not the rules for the construction of sentences, but "a system of agreements as to the relationship of words to bring about meaningful communication."

The distinction is enormously important and hits right at the heart of another formidable impediment to written and verbal expression: English grammar as a complex and ill-taught tradition. In the main, what passes for modern English usage is the legacy of medieval grammarians attempting to structure the language according to a Latin model. As part of the baggage comes a view of grammar as a stern subject to distinguish an elite from the vulgar. (Latin was, after all, both the language of the liturgy as well as diplomacy, and thus proper usage bore heavily upon social advancement. Moreover, the thirteenth-century grammarian counted himself as much a philosopher

as a linguist, and so offered his work as a highly esoteric study.) For all periodic talk of reformation, the trappings still remain. The modern grammarian is still a vaguely medieval figure, while his stock in trade is still an esoteric study of constricting rules. Then, too, those rules are still a fairly severe measure of social standing, and particularly so considering how difficult they are to comprehend.

What *The New Grammar* offers is basically the opposite—not a body of restrictive rules, but a means for limitless expression and perfect comprehension. In a concise explanation of his stance (and one drawn from the text itself), Ron writes: "It is particularly interesting to note that grammar is an after-the-fact subject. In other words, it seeks to make rules about something that has already been in use for ages and is in an evolved state. It does not create something. It merely tries to describe it.

"This immediately disposes of the idea that grammar is a *study* which belongs in the hands of the professors. It is obviously a *use* which belongs in the hands of the users. Written and spoken communication were not invented by grammarians. When grammarians do their job properly they assist people to understand each other in their written and spoken communication." Reflecting precisely that, and once more utilizing illustrations to teach, *The New Grammar* not only clarifies, but actually removes those elements of traditional grammar arbitrarily imposed upon the language for the sake of academic exercise. Thus comes a grammar truly of and for the people. Accordingly, *The New Grammar* is also an amazingly simple treatment of the subject and, in fact, represents the first complete and yet still comprehensible explanation of the way in which we use English.

What these three texts add up to, then, are students with the veritable key to English—how it is formed and how it is most effectively used for superior communication. For the younger student, Ron further offers his *How to Use a Dictionary* picture book for children and his *Grammar & Communication* for children. Yet in either case, the result is the same—an altogether remarkable command of the world's foremost language. That the author of these works was himself a world-renowned writer is to be expected. For what is ultimately offered here is nothing less than a writer's facility with the language...in all its power, its beauty and subtleties of phrasing. Needless to say, these works also provide a remarkable level of comprehension and, in fact, a passion for reading so deep and with such clarity that when placed in the hands of that grimly illiterate twenty-first-century student, we are honestly looking at the means for cultural renaissance. ■

"Grammar is established by common usage and forwarded by writers."

Thus Ron redefined grammar and thus he returned it to everyday people. Thus, too, he reintroduced the subject in his New Grammar book and so established it not as an academic study, but as a tool for communication. What follows, then, is his own prefatory note on grammar—its history, its function and its failings. While as a preliminary and all-encompassing word on the subject as a whole, he tells us with some emphasis:

"Grammar is something people need in order to understand and to be understood and that is the end of it."

GRAMMAR

by L. RON HUBBARD

"GRAMMAR" IS THE WAY words are organized into speech and writings so as to convey exact thoughts, ideas and meanings among people. It is essentially a system of agreements as to the relationship of words to bring about meaningful communication.

That is all that grammar is. If it is defined otherwise, students will think you are trying to teach them classroom rules, rather than how to talk and read.

You won't find this definition in dictionaries, because grammar fell into the hands of grammarians who themselves had a misunderstood on the word "grammar." It is that and that only which makes grammar tough. What you are trying to do is bypass the resulting complications.

Grammar is established by *common usage* and forwarded by *writers*. It got into a very dark eddy of a very dark river when it fell into the hands of the professors. This is basically what is wrong with it. It isn't even difficult to understand it. It is only difficult to understand the inability of the professors to write about it.

Grammar isn't the *study* of anything. It's the *use* of something. Now, a "professor" believes that anything is a study. That's because he gets paid for telling people it is a *study*. Grammar is a part of *everyday existence* and if you don't know it and can't use it, nobody can understand you and you can't understand others. And you would be in mystery about things and people a lot of the time.

If grammar is defined as the way words are organized into speech and writings so as to convey exact thoughts, ideas and meanings among people, students will be eager to study it rather than thinking they are suffering under the yoke of "professors" who themselves couldn't talk or communicate. Grammar is something people need in order to understand and to be understood and that is the end of it. *for*

Applied Scholastics International training campus at Spanish Lake, Missouri: providing instruction in all L. Ron Hubbard literacy tools and methodologies, Spanish Lake is now the wellspring of a Study Technology movement comprised of more than 120,000 educators

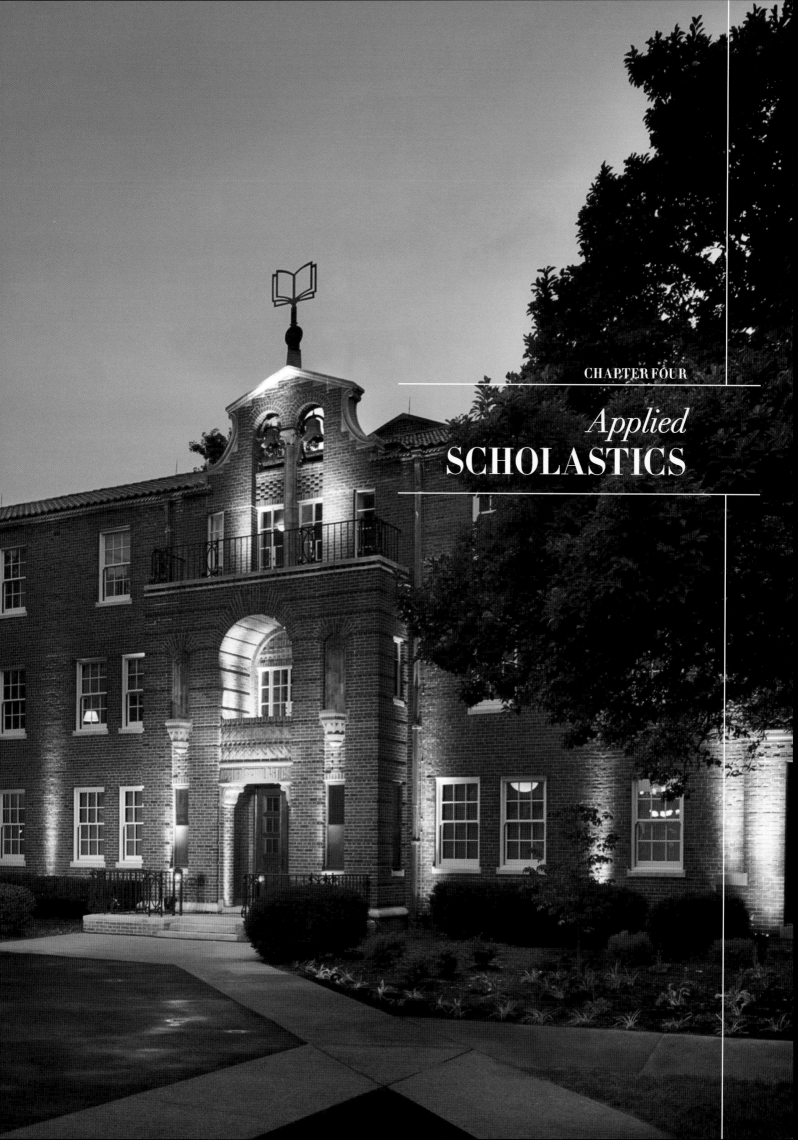

Applied
SCHOLASTICS

Applied
Scholastics

THE BROAD IMPLEMENTATION OF L. RON HUBBARD'S learning tools commenced in 1972 through Applied Scholastics International (APS). Founded by a consortium of American educators, Applied Scholastics, under the guidance of the Association for Better Living and Education, is dedicated to the worldwide dissemination of LRH educational technology. At the academic hub of the network stands the international training campus at Spanish Lake, Missouri. It is here educators world over acquire LRH literacy tools for application in every conceivable arena across some seventy nations. Indeed, and to date, Applied Scholastics brings L. Ron Hubbard's gift of learning to tens of thousands of instructors and many millions of students.

Initially, however, efforts remained focused on underprivileged students—most notably in South Africa, where L. Ron Hubbard had previously devoted considerable energy to improving township schools in the face of apartheid. At issue was a genuinely appalling double standard wherein native children were educated in only the loosest sense of the word. To cite just a few dire statistics: for every hundred black children entering native schools, only one finally qualified for higher education. Of those remaining, only four managed minimal diplomas from high school. Meanwhile another ten million children never spent a single day in class, prompting warnings of social upheaval and a lost generation.

In reply, however, L. Ron Hubbard study methods were brought to native schools in what he described as a spearheading basis. By 1975,

Left
The 2003 Grand Opening of the Applied Scholastics International training campus at Spanish Lake, Missouri

The Applied Scholastics campus at Spanish Lake, Missouri: worldwide hub of an academic movement exclusively devoted to L. Ron Hubbard's "technology for education" under an Applied Scholastics affiliate known as Education Alive, the program had come to embrace several districts to the benefit of many thousand students and instructors. Results are now regarded as legendary. Following a three-week course in LRH study methods, black teenagers from Transkei increased reading levels by more than *two years*. Moreover, a 15 percent failure rate at the Moretele College of Education fell to but 2 percent. There was still more at a Bapedi Lower Primary School, where a previously "impossible, retarded or bluntly stupid" class suddenly boasted test scores so superior to national norms educators were initially incredulous. In consequence, and fueled with corporate donations, Education Alive saw meteoric expansion until LRH learning tools were in the hands of some forty-five thousand instructors.

Elsewhere across the continent, the story of L. Ron Hubbard's Study Technology is no less dramatic. In classic grass-roots fashion, the movement swiftly spread to neighboring Zimbabwe, where yet another eighteen thousand educators immediately adopted LRH literacy tools for "greatly improved" comprehension among another one million students. The Gambia likewise followed suit, with national ministry implementation of Study Technology to boost previously languishing reading levels well above sub-Sahara norms.

There is altogether more wherever else students languish. Some thirty thousand scholastically challenged children from Puebla State schools in Mexico were presented with Study Technology. Immediately thereafter test scores soared twelve times national averages. In equally swift reply, the State Minister of Education doubled delivery resources under a declaration that reads: *"This is the solution Mexico needs!"*

The story of Study Technology is equally compelling in Venezuela, where 75 percent gains in student performance parallel a 90 percent reduction of schoolyard violence. While if only to emphasize the diversity, L. Ron Hubbard's educational texts topped national bestseller lists in the ever-competitive Japan.

The story of Study Technology in ailing American schools is no less illuminating. A Supplementary Educational Service Provider under the No Child Left Behind Act, Applied Scholastics trainers enjoy an unprecedented record in salvaging "critical list" schools. The case in point was a Memphis, Tennessee, high school facing imminent federal cuts and likely closure unless scholastic performance was radically improved. Accordingly, the Applied

Scholastics rescue mission performed what amounted to scholastic resuscitation with Study Technology across the whole curriculum. What ensued is what has been dubbed the "Memphis Miracle" inasmuch as the APS adopted school was the *only* institution in the district to graduate from federal critical lists. Moreover—and here, too, is an APS trademark—the feat was accomplished in less than twenty hours of tutoring, after which reading levels rose more than two scholastic grades.

There is many another exemplary story from Applied Scholastics case files. Some three hundred Tennessee high-school students were similarly resuscitated in but five weeks of Study Technology tutoring; whereupon 97.5 percent passed the standardized tests district supervisors were certain they would fail.

The case files are equally graphic when discussing inner-city schools across the Los Angeles basin. To cite the dire statistics here: schools suffer dropout rates as high as 60 percent, leaving just under half those of high-school age functionally illiterate. (The figures significantly rise when discussing members of the various Compton street gangs—which, incidentally, says something about the regular threats of physical violence leveled at inner-city teachers and thus the "high-risk" status of Compton instructors.)

Not so easily measured, but just as integral to the problem, is what community leaders describe as a rock-bottom despair—the fact that a significant proportion of Compton youth could not fill out an employment application and life expectancy of an inner-city "warrior" was but twenty or so years...unless, of course, he is removed from the streets to serve a double-digit prison term.

Yet into this dead end of Western academia came LRH Study Technology under a Compton Literacy and Learning Project. The aim was the intellectual salvation of at-risk youth and particularly those from notoriously violent neighborhood gangs. As a further word on the matter, and a vital one, project founders described their mission as "the fundamental of all fundamentals." That is, one may glibly speak of economic aid to disadvantaged black communities, "but let's first teach them to read." To precisely that end, Compton instructors introduced L. Ron Hubbard's *How to Use a Dictionary* picture book for children and *Grammar & Communication* for children.

Above top The Applied Scholastics training campus at Spanish Lake, Missouri, welcomes educators from some fifty nations and every conceivable academic arena

Above bottom Through an Applied Scholastics Achievement Program, senior educators become Study Technology specialists who, in turn, train colleagues across their respective school systems. In this way, L. Ron Hubbard's learning and literacy tools are now at work on behalf of millions.

Right The Central Lecture Hall at Spanish Lake, site of Applied Scholastics symposiums attracting an international assembly of educators from every academic echelon—quite literally from kindergarten teachers to Ministers of Education

Results were again both swift and dramatic. Compton youths typically gained two academic years for every twenty hours of tutoring, prompting a deputy director from the National Institute for Literacy to describe the program as working "where the rubber meets the road in terms of solving illiteracy problems in America."

Applied Scholastics   95

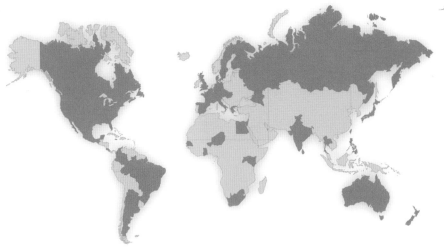

Individual stories are even more compelling:

- Once seriously vicious gang members were soon tutoring those from rival factions who, in turn, signed on as tutors themselves.

- A once incorrigible "gangbanger" was writing: *"I now know why you want us to do this course. You want us to do this course, because words are power. And if you know the words, you don't need to use guns."*

- A once wholly illiterate drug dealer was writing: *"Between heaven and earth there is a place where spiritual wholeness can be embraced."*

- A previously homeless and illiterate cocaine addict landed his first steady job, rented his first apartment and, in something of a landmark decision, recovered custody of his daughter from a foster home, with college-level reading skills.

Thereafter, the project became what it is today: the World Literacy Crusade with sister programs across the United States, Canada, Great Britain, Australia, New Zealand, India and Malaysia. A similarly aimed project in Hollywood gained funding from the California Governor's Office when police reported direct correlations between rising literacy rates of at-risk youth and plummeting juvenile crime rates. The project further earned the President of the United States' Community Volunteer Award, after which it extended to cities across North America, Great Britain and Africa.

Likewise now comprising an extracurricular learning network are the nearly two dozen centers of Denmark's Association for Effective Basic Education. As elsewhere, the Danish centers are regularly called upon to salvage failing students from the public school system, thereby reaffirming what Applied Scholastics tutorial programs represent as the measurable bottom line in remedial education.

The story grows even more expansive when L. Ron Hubbard's educational technology is put to work across entire curriculums. The Applied Scholastics network of schools presents Study Technology in full throughout all courses of study. The hallmark example is the Delphi network, with campuses from Oregon and California to Florida and Massachusetts. Extending from kindergarten through high school, Delphi Academies provide what all better private schools advertise: an atmosphere conducive to excellence, greater individual attention and generally superior faculties. Yet with a strict adherence to L. Ron Hubbard's

Study Technology in every aspect of instruction, Delphi does much more. In point of fact, the Delphi student routinely leads contemporaries as measured by standardized aptitude tests and otherwise scores higher than all national norms. Moreover, and even if difficult to measure statistically, the Delphi student is a genuinely enthusiastic learner. To be sure—and this from an independent study conducted in coordination with the United States Department of Education:

"Mr. Hubbard's contributions to educational methodology reflect current research on what we know about how people learn. This application allows students to become more accountable, self-directed and self-advocating, while teaching them strategies and skills to help them think, learn and develop more of their potential over an entire lifetime."

Although fairly obvious, it might further be mentioned the Delphi campus is both drug-free and violence-free.

The story is repeated wherever one finds Applied Scholastics schools: in Copenhagen's Amager's International School, where students from scores of nations now study according to the L. Ron Hubbard method and all under Danish government funding; in England's Greenfields School, where a traditional British education has been augmented with Study Technology for more than two decades and Virginia's Chesapeake Ability School, where students typically score several hundred points above national averages on Scholastic Aptitude Tests.

All of which returns us to the international training campus helming the APS network at Spanish Lake, Missouri. It was expressly designed to meet global demands for Study Technology and provides educators with the training to implement that technology in their own schools/universities. Given what LRH educational technology further represents across the rest of the learning community, Spanish Lake is additionally geared to the corporate trainer, the community tutor and educational consultant. Indeed, and regardless of the labels with which our educational failures are so conveniently dismissed, Spanish Lake stands affirmation of the fact anyone can better comprehend the written word with L. Ron Hubbard's educational technology. ∎

For L. Ron Hubbard's contributions to education and literacy come the awards and recognitions from every academic corner. Of particular note are those from developing-world arenas where more than one educator now proclaims, "The hope of making a great nation is now possible with Study Technology."

Epilogue

"We are living in an age of widespread illiteracy," L. Ron Hubbard reminds us, and the consequences are grave. In addition to the obvious repercussions of lost productivity, we must finally come to terms with at least two generations unable to comprehend or communicate in any meaningful way. We must further come to terms with that grimmest of nongraduating classes—listless from drugs, dull-eyed from television and video games, possessing not the faintest conception of history, mathematics, fine art or literature and yet, on occasion, unimaginably violent.

At the same time, however, let us try and grasp the full significance of this closing statement: Having engaged in a study of illiteracy, illiterate and semiliterate populations, L. Ron Hubbard has provided the solutions to a worldwide educational crisis. Those solutions allow for the total comprehension of any subject; they are easily learned and applied and are otherwise available to all who would reach for them.

APPENDIX

GLOSSARY

A

abdominal: relating to, located in or occurring in the *abdomen,* the part of the body containing the stomach, intestines and other organs. Page 76.

abiding: continuing, steadfast, unwavering. Page 18.

abounded in: contained (something) in large numbers or amounts. Page 59.

abstract: based on general principles or theories rather than on specific instances. Page 19.

academia: the world of learning, teaching, research, etc., at universities and the people involved in it. Page 11.

academic: of or relating to a school or other educational institutions. Page 3.

acclaim: enthusiastic approval given to somebody or something publicly. Page 1.

accountable: responsible or answerable for something, as for one's conduct. Page 97.

ache: feel eager or want to do something very much. Page 59.

adaption: the act of taking up or of changing a plan, idea, cause or practice to suit particular conditions or a particular purpose. Page 64.

adept: very skilled; expert. Page 5.

adjustment, social: the process of modifying, adapting or altering individual or collective patterns of behavior to bring them into conformity with other such patterns, as with those provided by a cultural environment. Page 12.

adolescent: relating to the period of *adolescence,* the time of developing from a younger to an adult stage. Also, an individual in this time period. Page 3.

advancement, social: the promotion of a person so that he assumes a higher rank or status in society. Page 84.

Adventure: an American pulp magazine founded in 1910 and published mostly as a monthly magazine until 1971. In addition to adventure and fiction stories, the magazine had other features, including a column for readers to write to and a question-and-answer service. Page 20.

affect: adopt a use, style or manner as one's own. Page 62.

affiliate(s): a branch or unit of a larger organization. Page 92.

affinity: a natural liking for or attraction to a person, thing, idea, etc. Page 45.

affirmation, stands: acts as a demonstration or evidence of the truth of a statement. Page 97.

Agana: former name of *Hagatna,* the capital of Guam, located on the western coast of the island. Page 11.

alignment: a state of being properly coordinated or being in agreement with. Page 59.

allied: associated or connected, especially by common properties or similar characteristics. Page 57.

alter ego: in psychoanalysis, a second self. A term sometimes used to refer to the opposite side of a personality. Page 16.

amar (amo, amas): different forms of the Spanish verb meaning love: *amar,* to love; *amo,* I love; *amas,* you love. Page 32.

American University: a private university in Washington, DC, founded in 1893. It offers courses in a broad range of fields, including arts and sciences, communications, public affairs, business administration and law. Page 82.

amount to: develop into; become. Page 21.

anecdote: a short account of a particular incident or event of an interesting or amusing nature, often biographical. Page 11.

animal husbandry: the science of breeding, feeding and tending domestic animals. Page 28.

animated: made to move or give the appearance of moving as if alive. Page 14.

antipathy: a feeling of strong dislike or hostility; a fixed opposition directed toward (someone or something). Page 45.

apartheid: (in the Republic of South Africa) a rigid policy of political and economic discrimination and segregation of the nonwhite population, in effect from 1948 to 1991. Page 91.

Apostle Paul: a first-century leader of Christianity and prominent *apostle,* an early follower of Jesus who carried the Christian message into the world. Paul was a missionary in regions around Israel and in parts of Greece. Page 24.

Applied Scholastics International: an association of educators founded in 1972 and dedicated to the worldwide dissemination of LRH educational technology. From its central training campus in Spanish Lake, a community located near St. Louis, Missouri, and through local chapters throughout the world, Applied Scholastics provides educators, governments, community groups, parents and students with the learning tools they need to achieve a world free from illiteracy, where individuals know how to learn and can achieve their chosen goals. Page 88.

appointed: selected to do a particular job. Page 67.

arbitrary: based on personal decision or random choice rather than on any rules, principles or system. Page 4.

arena: a field of interest, activity or the like. Page 4.

armed to the teeth: fully equipped with what is considered needful. *To the teeth* means lacking nothing, completely. Figuratively, someone who looks *armed to the teeth* would be someone who looks fully prepared to accomplish something. Page 76.

Army Alfa: also *Army Alpha* or the *Alpha Examination,* a timed test developed during World War I (1914–1918) and used by the United States Army in testing recruits for general intelligence and ability. Page 56.

arrogant: unpleasantly proud and behaving as if one knows more or is more important than other people. Page 70.

article: a word that tells whether a speaker or writer is referring to a specific person, place or thing (for example, *the* dog) or whether he's referring to any one person, place or thing out of a general group (for example, *a* dog). Page 44.

articles, quality group: stories produced for the top-ranked pulp magazines, viewed as the "quality group" of magazines because they published the best writing by the most accomplished writers. Page 21.

articulate: able to express oneself easily and use language with clarity and effectiveness. Page 75.

ascertain: find out definitely; learn with certainty or assurance; determine. Page 64.

as it were: if one might so put it; a phrase used to indicate that a word or statement is perhaps not formally exact though practically right. Page 14.

assertion: something stated positively. Page 59.

assimilate: absorb as one's own; take into the mind and thoroughly understand. Page 11.

associate professor: an academic ranking immediately below full professor, the highest rank. Page 82.

association: the connection or relation of ideas, feelings, sensations; correlation of the elements of perception, reasoning or the like. Page 10.

Association for Better Living and Education (ABLE): an international nonprofit public benefit corporation formed in 1988 and dedicated to social betterment. ABLE is empowered to authorize qualified social betterment groups to use L. Ron Hubbard's technologies in purely secular charitable and educational activities. From its headquarters in Los Angeles, California, and through regional groups located throughout the world, ABLE sees that LRH solutions are implemented for raising public morals, increasing adherence to human rights, rehabilitating lives through drug and criminal reform and improving education through use of LRH Study Technology. Page 91.

Attention Deficit Disorder: a psychiatric label for a supposed disorder (illness) applied to persons, mainly children, who have a deficit (lack) in the ability to focus attention and who are considered hyperactive (too active). Also called *Attention Deficit Hyperactivity Disorder (ADHD).* Page 4.

augmented: made (something already developed) greater, as in size, extent or quantity. Page 97.

aversion: an intense or definite feeling of dislike. Page 59.

avid: eager for or enthusiastic about something. Page 65.

axioms: statements of natural laws on the order of those of the physical sciences. Page 36.

B

baffled: confused; unable to understand or explain something. Page 33.

baffling: confusing in a way that prevents understanding or solving; puzzling. Page 77.

baggage: things that block progress, development, ability to use new information or the like. Page 27.

Bapedi Lower Primary School: a school for younger children, located in Soweto, a black community created during the apartheid era, now forming a part of Johannesburg, South Africa. Page 92.

barge: a flat-bottomed vessel for transporting large quantities of freight, especially on rivers or canals. Page 11.

Barnaby Rudge: a historical novel by the English author Charles Dickens, a story of religious controversy set in England in the late 1700s. Page 33.

batteries: any large groups or series of related things. Page 44.

beach, on the: badly needing money or work; unemployed and having no money. Literally, *on the beach* means on land, hence not aboard ship and not employed. Page 32.

bear upon: relate to or affect (something). Page 4.

bedrock: the fundamental principles forming a firm foundation on which something is based. From the unbroken, solid rock that underlies the soil on the surface of the Earth. Page 47.

befallen: happened to or occurred. Page 41.

behavioral school: a branch of psychology based on the observation of how people behave and using methods that attempt to change behavior. Page 13.

behaviorist: of or relating to the behavioral school of psychology. *See also* **behavioral school.** Page 14.

bellow: shout something in a loud, deep voice. Page 20.

belt, under (one's): done, experienced or acquired something that will be of benefit to one in the future. Page 15.

Berber: a people that have inhabited large sections of North Africa since the earliest recorded time. References to them date from about 3000 B.C. and occur frequently in ancient Egyptian, Greek and Roman sources. For many centuries the Berbers inhabited the coast of North Africa from Egypt to the Atlantic Ocean. Page 75.

beside: 1. other than; except, as in *"Beside yourself, no other man there had anything to say other than dry, textbook things."* Page 20.
2. over and above; in addition to, as in *"wanting something beside a Latin conjugation."* Page 21.

bewilderment: the state or condition of being completely confused or puzzled. Page 29.

biology: the science of the origin, development, physical characteristics, habits, etc., of living forms. Page 28.

bitt: a strong post on a wharf or on the deck of a ship, used for securing ropes. Page 28.

blood and thunder: a story that has exaggerated drama, violence and uproar. The phrase comes from blood (bloodshed) and thunder (violence). Page 20.

blunt: direct and straightforward. Page 60.

boards, by the: be lost, neglected or destroyed. The term *boards* in nautical language refers to the side of a wooden sailing ship, and the phrase *by the board* originated in the days of sailing ships when in the height of a storm, a mast was broken and it was up to the skipper to either save it or let it go by the board—fall over the side of the ship to destruction. Page 31.

bogs (someone): mires (someone) down, sinks (someone) in, or as if in, a bog (wet, spongy ground). Page 59.

bombardment: the act of being persistently subjected to a stream of something. Page 33.

books: the written records of money that a business has spent or received. Page 33.

bore upon: related to or affected something. Page 84.

Bostonian: a person who lives in Boston, a seaport in and the capital of Massachusetts, a state located in the northeastern part of the United States. Page 65.

bottom-line: of or having to do with the *bottom line,* the fundamental and deciding factor in any situation. Literally, the line at the bottom of a financial report showing the final profit or loss that a company makes at the end of a given period of time. Page 47.

bountifully: with plentiful supply; abundantly. Page 64.

bowing to: accepting something and yielding to it, often unwillingly. Page 65.

brain-cracking: extremely difficult to understand or causing great strain on one's mind, due to being complex, confusing, etc. Page 59.

breadth: extent or range of something. Page 54.

bright spot: a good or pleasant part of something that is unpleasant or bad in all other ways. Page 18.

Browning, Robert: (1812–1889) English poet, noted for his finely drawn character studies in a style of poetry he developed called *dramatic monologues.* In these poems, Browning speaks in the voice of an imaginary or historical character at a dramatic moment in that person's life. Page 18.

Bruner, Jerome: (1915–) American psychologist and educator, a leading figure in the study of perception and language development. Page 17.

buff(s): someone who is enthusiastic about and has a wide knowledge of a particular subject. Page 69.

bugbear: a persistent problem or source of annoyance. Page 32.

building block: literally, a large block of concrete or similar hard material used for building houses and other large structures. Hence anything thought of as a basic unit of construction, such as an element or component regarded as contributing to something's growth or development. Page 44.

burgeoning: experiencing growth; developing. Page 16.

bypass: avoid (something) by using an alternative channel, passage or route. Page 87.

by way of: by means of; by the route of. Page 43.

C

calculus: a form of mathematics used to make calculations dealing with things in a state of change. In calculus, irregular shapes can be measured or the rate of speed of an accelerating rocket can be determined. Page 11.

Calculus Made Easy: a book on calculus originally published in 1910 by Silvanus P. Thompson (British physicist and scientific writer). It is considered a classic and elegant introduction to the subject and remains one of the most popular texts on calculus ever written. Page 29.

capsule: enclose in or as if in a *capsule,* a compact and movable container, case or envelope. Page 64.

case in point: a relevant example or illustration of something. Page 92.

caste: a social class separated from others by distinctions of hereditary rank, profession or wealth. Page 36.

casting about: going around or searching for something. Page 23.

cataloging: systematically arranging and listing. Page 64.

catapult: literally, a device that can throw objects at a high speed. Used figuratively. Page 19.

catchphrase: a phrase that attracts or is supposed to attract broad attention. Page 3.

ccs.: an abbreviation for *cubic centimeters,* a unit of measure of volume equivalent to that of a cube 1 centimeter × 1 centimeter × 1 centimeter. A *centimeter* is equivalent to 0.3937 inch. Page 22.

Chamorro: of the native peoples of Guam and the Mariana Islands, in the western Pacific Ocean. Guam is the largest and southernmost of the Mariana Islands. The Mariana Islands extend north 1,565 miles (2,500 kilometers) from Guam almost to Japan. Page 9.

Chandler, Raymond: (1888–1959) American author of crime and detective stories, mostly set in Los Angeles during the 1930s and 1940s. Page 14.

channel(s): a method or system that is used to communicate with people or to get something done. Page 28.

character: the set of qualities that make someone distinctive, especially someone's qualities of mind and feeling. Page 68.

characterization: the way in which a writer portrays the characters (people represented in a film, play or story), especially in such a way as to make them seem real. Page 15.

characters, Chinese: the symbols of the Chinese writing system, derived from picture writing. Page 62.

Chaucer: Geoffrey Chaucer (1340?–1400), outstanding English poet of the Middle Ages, whose works formed a major influence on the development of English literature. Page 60.

"chicken-and-egg" question: an apparently unresolvable problem regarding which of two parts came first or which part caused the other. The expression comes from the literal example of this problem expressed by a chicken and an egg, as follows: to have a chicken, it must have come from an egg; but, to have an egg, there must have first been a chicken that laid the egg. The question, then, is which came first—the chicken or the egg? Page 77.

chilling: causing a feeling of dread or horror. Page 2.

chronometer: an instrument for measuring time precisely; a highly accurate kind of clock, as for use in navigation. Page 16.

circa: used before a date to indicate that it is approximate or estimated; approximately. Page 75.

claptrap: important-sounding nonsense; insincere or empty language. Page 4.

classics: books, plays, poetry or other writing that is well known and considered to be of very high quality, setting standards for other books, etc. Page 9.

clipped: (of a word or expression) shortened by abbreviating it or dropping a syllable. Page 67.

code(s): any system of symbols for meaningful communication, such as a *phonetic code,* a set of symbols in which each symbol represents an exact speech sound. *See also* **phonetic.** Page 77.

cold, left (one): did not make (one) feel interested, impressed or the like. Page 21.

cold war: hostilities short of armed conflict that existed after World War II (1939–1945) between the Soviet Union and countries supporting the communist system, and the democratic countries of the Western world under the leadership of the United States. Page 17.

colonial: a person who lives in a colony (a group of people who settle in a distant land under the government of their native land). Page 65.

colony: a group of individuals living in close association and dependent on each other. Page 13.

colored: influenced or distorted to some degree; caused to appear different from what something really is or should be. Page 64.

column left: a command used in marching to execute a turn to the left. A *column* is a formation of troops consisting of a long, moving line. Page 22.

combustion: the act or process of burning. Page 52.

commencement: a ceremony during which students formally receive their degrees, or the day on which this ceremony takes place. Page 24.

commensurate: corresponding in extent or degree; proportionate. Page 2.

commissioner: a government official or representative in charge of a department or district. Page 35.

commonweal: the common welfare; the public good. Page 12.

communication: an interchange of ideas between two or more people. Page 4.

Community Volunteer Award: also called the *President's Volunteer Service Award,* a program established on a national level to honor Americans who volunteer their time to help improve their communities. The award, consisting of a pin, a certificate and a note of congratulations from the president of the United States, is given to individuals and groups that have demonstrated outstanding volunteer service for their communities during a twelve-month period. Page 96.

compelling: exerting a strong and irresistible effect, influence, etc. Page 92.

complication(s): a secondary disease or condition aggravating an already existing one. Page 76.

component(s): a part or division of something; an element of a larger whole or something bigger. Page 4.

Compton: a city and suburb of Los Angeles, California. Page 93.

computation: the processing of data to come up with answers; calculation. Page 37.

conceptual(ly): relating to concepts (something formed in the mind; a general idea or thought) or to the forming of concepts. Page 45.

conjugation: the arrangement of forms of verbs for different uses. For example, one part of the conjugation of the verb *to be* includes these forms: *I was, he was, you were, they were.* Page 21.

conjunction: a word or words that join words or groups of words. For example, in the sentence "Bill and Max are carrying a box," the conjunction *and* joins together the two names, *Bill* and *Max.* Page 44.

consigned: transferred to another's custody or charge; entrusted. Page 17.

consortium: any association, partnership or union. Page 91.

constricting: slowing or stopping the natural course or development of. Page 82.

contemporary: characteristic of the present period; modern; current. Page 41.

context: the words or passages of text that come before or after a particular word that help to explain or determine its full meaning; the general sense of a word or a clarification of it. Page 51.

control group: a group of individuals not using some procedure as compared with those who do use it, created to correctly compare and contrast the results of a test. Page 46.

conversely: in a way that is opposite to what has just been stated. Page 44.

coos: makes a soft murmuring sound. Page 31.

Copenhagen: capital and largest city of Denmark, located on two neighboring islands in the eastern part of the country. Page 97.

copperplate: an elegant style of handwriting that became popular in the 1700s, characterized by a slant to the right, regular loops and vertical strokes that are thicker than the horizontal strokes. Taught to schoolchildren in Europe and the United States during the 1700s and 1800s, copperplate was based on models of handwriting created by masters in the seventeenth and eighteenth centuries. Their works were engraved on polished copper printing plates (hence the name). Page 67.

copy: the written text to be published in a book, newspaper or magazine, as distinct from visual material or graphics. Page 67.

copywriter: somebody who writes the texts for advertisements and other publicity material. Page 64.

corporate trainer: a person working in a business or other organization and responsible for training staff, both in specific skills needed for their positions and in social skills such as effective communication, leadership, etc. Page 97.

correlate: establish or indicate the proper relation between. Page 22.

crammed: stuffed, especially forcibly, into something. Page 22.

crane forward: stretch the neck forward to hear or see something better. Page 69.

cranium: the skull, specifically the part of the skull that encloses the brain. Page 33.

credit hour: recognition at a school or college that represents one hour of classroom study per week over the period of time that the course is taught. Page 21.

credit rating: a reference to the action of officially recognizing a person or organization as having met a standard or criterion. Page 29.

creed: any codification of belief or of opinion. Page 13.

crusade: a vigorous, aggressive action for the defense or advancement of an idea, cause, etc. Page 62.

cult: great or excessive devotion or dedication to some person, idea or thing. Page 12.

cultured: improved by education; having refined taste, speech and manners. Page 70.

curls: fancy curves, spiral lines or the like, as in some handwriting styles, especially as found on capital letters or other parts of a document made more noticeable. Page 67.

curriculum: the whole of the series of courses of study given in a school, college, university, etc. Also, the elements taught in a particular subject. In plural form, *curricula*. Page 10.

curve: a graphic representation of the variations caused in something by changing conditions, often drawn as a curve. Page 28.

custody: the legal right and responsibility for raising a child and seeing to the child's upbringing, especially the right to keep the child in one's home. Page 96.

D

dams up: holds back or obstructs (something). A *dam* is literally a barrier (usually of concrete) constructed to hold back water. Page 62.

Dark Age: a period of severe decline within a civilization and one that is without knowledge or culture; a period characterized by lack of intellectual and spiritual activity. Likened to the roughly thousand-year period in European history dating from the A.D. 400s, specifically the intellectual darkness, such as lack of learning and schooling during this period, the loss of many artistic and technical skills, and the virtual disappearance of the knowledge held by previous Greek and Roman civilizations. Page 2.

dead reckoning: a simple method of determining the position of a ship or aircraft by charting its course and speed from a previously known position. (Also called *ded-reckoning, ded* being short for *deduced,* arrived at by reasoning.) Page 16.

dean: an official of a school, college or university, especially one in charge of students, faculty or a division of studies. Page 15.

declared: openly stated or made known. Page 5.

definitive: having a fixed and final form; providing a solution or final answer; satisfying all requirements. Page 46.

deign: do something in a way that shows that one considers it a great favor and almost beneath one's dignity to do it. Page 65.

delineation: description or precise outlining of something. Page 4.

Department of Education, United States: an executive department of the United States Government, created in 1979 from earlier federal departments that had included education since the mid-nineteenth century. The purpose of the department is to ensure equal educational opportunity for all and to improve the quality of that education through federal support, research programs and information sharing. Page 97.

Department of Labor, United States: an executive department of the United States Government, created in 1913, with the stated purpose "to foster, promote and develop the welfare of the wage earners of the United States, to improve their working conditions and to advance their opportunities for profitable employment." Page 75.

derivation symbols: any symbols, abbreviations or the like used in presenting data about a *derivation,* the origin and development of a word showing how it has arrived at its current form and meaning. These could include symbols such as + (to show that a word is made up of two parts) or < (to show that a word comes from an earlier word) or abbreviations of names of languages, etc. Page 77.

Detective Fiction Weekly: a pulp magazine that published some nine hundred issues in all, from the early 1920s until the early 1950s, containing stories by many of the best-known authors of stories for the pulp magazines. Page 20.

developing solutions: chemical solutions used in developing film. *Develop* means place film that has been exposed to light (as when a photograph is taken) into various liquids to make the picture visible. When film is exposed to light, it records an invisible image on the film. The film is put through a series of chemical baths that cause the image on the exposed film to become visible as a negative. The film is then allowed to dry. The negative can now be used to make a print of the photograph. Page 41.

Dewey: John Dewey (1859–1952), American philosopher, educator and author who was strongly influenced by modern psychology and the theory of evolution. The poor performance of today's educational system has been traced by many to changes introduced by Dewey. Page 12.

dialect: a form of a language or manner of speaking (written and spoken) that is specific to, or characteristic of, a specific region or social group. Page 64.

Dianetics: Dianetics is a forerunner and substudy of Scientology. Dianetics means "through the mind" or "through the soul" (from Greek *dia,* through, and *nous,* mind or soul). It is a system of coordinated axioms which resolve problems concerning human behavior and psychosomatic illnesses. It combines a workable technique and a thoroughly validated method for increasing sanity, by erasing unwanted sensations and unpleasant emotions. Page 1.

Dianetics: The Modern Science of Mental Health: the bestselling book by L. Ron Hubbard, first published in 1950. It is the basic text on Dianetics and gives the theory and practice of the subject. Page 36.

Dickens: Charles Dickens (1812–1870), prolific English novelist of the mid-nineteenth century whose books are noted for picturesque and extravagant characters in the lower economic strata of England. Page 33.

diction: vocal expression, especially clear, accurate and pleasing delivery in speech. Page 57.

diffident: restrained or reserved in manner, conduct, etc. Page 62.

diplomacy: the conduct by government officials of negotiations and other relations between nations. Page 84.

disability: an inability to perform particular activities. Page 4.

disdain: a feeling that someone or something is unworthy of one's consideration or respect; haughty (arrogantly superior) disrespect or indifference. Page 57.

disorder: a condition involving a disturbance of the normal functioning of the mind or body. Page 4.

disreputable: dishonest and bad. Page 60.

dissertation: a spoken or written communication about a subject, in which it is discussed at length. Page 18.

distinction: 1. the separation of people into various groups. Hence *"wipe out race and class distinctions"* refers to no longer separating people into groups based on race or class. Page 56.
2. a clear difference, or the recognition of a difference, between things that are similar or related. Page 84.

domain: territory ruled by a government. Page 10.

doors have closed no more...: the doors of a university are no longer confining one within or being entered through; that is, one is no longer attending classes. Page 19.

double standard: any code or set of principles containing different provisions for one group of people than for another. Page 91.

dour: sullen; gloomy. Page 3.

draft: the depth of water needed for a boat to float, often marked on the side of a vessel as a scale of feet. This enables the weight or quantity, as of cargo, to be estimated by how low the boat rides in the water as observed on the scale. Page 28.

drawing upon: using or making use of, especially as a source or resource for something; obtaining from (a particular source). Page 1.

dropout rate: the percentage of dropouts (students leaving school before completing a course of instruction) in a particular period. Page 45.

dry: dull, boring. Page 20.

dryad: in Greek mythology, a spiritual being believed to live in trees and forests. Page 31.

Du Bois, W.E.B.: William Edward Burghardt Du Bois (1868–1963), US historian, author, educator and a leading black opponent of racial discrimination. Along with teaching and writing, Du Bois supported civil rights causes and helped found the National Association for the Advancement of Colored People (NAACP). Page 93.

dynamic range: the range in volume between the high points and the low points of a program. (The meaning of *dynamic* in this context is relating to or indicating variations in the loudness of sounds.) Page 68.

dysfunctional: unable to deal adequately with normal social relations. Page 76.

E

eccentric: deviating from what is usual, ordinary or customary, as in conduct or manner; odd; unconventional. Page 18.

echo reflection: a sound that is heard after it has been reflected off (thrown back away from) a surface such as a wall. These sounds then travel back to the listener. The echo is similar to, but not the same as, the original sound. Page 70.

eddy: a movement in a flowing stream, as of water, in which the current doubles back to form a small whirl. Page 87.

educational psychologist: someone who studies *educational psychology,* a branch of psychology concerned with developing supposedly effective educational techniques and dealing with psychological problems in schools. Page 12.

egalitarian: marked by the belief that people are equal in worth and are entitled to equal access to the rights and privileges of their society. Page 4.

ego: in psychoanalysis, that part of the mind which is said to experience the external world through the senses and to rationally organize thought processes and govern action. *Ego* is Latin for "I." Page 16.

elocution: the art of public speaking so far as it regards delivery, pronunciation, tones and gestures; manner or style of oral delivery. Page 57.

embodied: included or contained as a part. Page 44.

embrace: accept or support (a belief or change) willingly. Page 13.

emeritus: retired or honorably discharged from active professional duty but retaining the title of one's office or position. Page 24.

eminence: superiority in rank, position, character, achievement, etc.; greatness. Page 27.

empowered: given ability; enabled. Page 5.

encoded: prepared in the form of a *code,* a system of words that are used symbolically to convey meaning beyond what is literally represented in the text. Page 18.

engendered: brought about; produced. Page 3.

entrance: permission to enter and be enrolled as a student in a school, usually granted by passing an examination and certain requirements of past studies and grades. Page 56.

enunciation: the action of pronouncing something distinctly. Page 65.

equitable: of actions, arrangements, decisions, etc., that is fair to all concerned; just. Page 1.

errata sheet: *errata* are lists of errors and their corrections. An *errata sheet* may be a loose leaf inserted into a book or placed in the book before the book is bound. Page 67.

erudite: knowledgeable; having or showing great knowledge gained from study and reading. Page 54.

esoteric: beyond the understanding or knowledge of most people. Page 84.

et al.: abbreviation for the Latin phrase *et alia,* meaning "and others." Page 29.

Ethics Resource Center: a nonprofit research organization dedicated to independent research that advances high ethical standards and practices in public and private institutions. Founded in 1922, the Ethics Resource Center is located in Arlington, Virginia. Page 2.

ethnological: of or having to do with *ethnology,* the science that analyzes cultures, especially in regard to their historical development and the similarities and dissimilarities between them. Page 14.

evaluate: work out or measure the value of. Page 37.

evolutionary parts, sum of his: a total of separate things that have come about because of *evolution,* a very ancient theory that all plants and animals developed from simpler forms and were shaped by their surroundings rather than being planned or created. Page 13.

exasperated: very angry or frustrated. Page 11.

"Excalibur": a philosophic manuscript written by L. Ron Hubbard in 1938. Although unpublished as such, the body of information it contained has since been released in various Dianetics and Scientology materials. (*Excalibur* was the name of the magic sword of King Arthur, legendary British hero, said to have ruled in the fifth or sixth century A.D.) Page 26.

exhortation: an urgent appeal or warning. Page 24.

extracurricular: done or happening outside of one's regular study or program of courses. Page 13.

F

facility: the quality, fact or condition of being easy or easily performed; freedom from difficulty. Page 85.

faction: a group of persons forming a cohesive, usually quarrelsome, minority within a larger group. Page 96.

fact-laden: filled with or having a lot of facts. Page 22.

factoring into: being included as an essential element, especially in the planning of something. Page 3.

fascist: one who practices *fascism,* a governmental system led by a dictator having complete power, which forcibly suppresses opposition and criticism and regiments all industry, commerce, etc. Page 64.

fell into the hands of: came under the influence, power or control of. Page 87.

fine art(s): any of the various arts (painting, music, sculpture, drawing, watercolor, graphics or architecture) considered to have been created primarily for aesthetic purposes and judged for beauty and meaningfulness. *Fine* means excellent or admirable. Page 101.

first-world: of or relating to the principal industrialized countries of the world. Page 2.

Fla.: an abbreviation for *Florida. See also* **Florida.** Page 24.

flame out, take the: do away with angry words (as in an argument). Figuratively, *flame* is an intense emotion, such as anger or passion, likened to the flames of a fire. Page 59.

flatboat: a large, flat-bottomed boat for use in shallow water, especially on rivers. Page 60.

Florida: a state in the southeastern United States, lying mostly on a peninsula between the Atlantic Ocean and the Gulf of Mexico. Page 96.

football: also called *American football,* a game that originated in the United States in the late 1860s. It is played by two opposing teams of eleven players each, using an inflated oval ball made of a rubber bag encased in leather. The object of the game is to move the ball, mainly by running with it and passing it, past the other team's goal posts, which counts as a score. Page 12.

footing: the basis on which something is established or operates. Page 59.

forebear(s): a member of past generations, as of a group or race. Page 13.

foregone conclusion: a decision or opinion formed in advance of proper consideration or full evidence. Page 21.

foreshadow: a technique said to be used by some writers, as in short stories, novels or the like, to give the reader hints or suggestions about coming action. It is used to develop expectancy in a reader by giving clues as to what is about to happen. *Foreshadow* literally means a shadow cast before an object. Page 15.

form: the customary or correct method or procedure. Page 12.

formidable: challenging or appearing to be overwhelming. Page 84.

formula(s): in mathematics, a rule or principle represented in symbols, numbers or letters, often equating one thing to another. Example: A + 4 = 7. From this one can figure out that A = 3. Page 21.

foster home: a home and parental care and upbringing provided to a child, usually on a short-term basis, by persons (foster parents) who are not related to the child by blood or adoption. A foster home is for children whose natural parents are dead, absent or unfit or unable to look after them. Page 96.

fraternity: a social society for men who are students at a college or university. Page 12.

freshman: a student in the first year of college in the United States. Page 13.

Freud, Sigmund: (1856–1939) Austrian founder of psychoanalysis who emphasized that unconscious memories of a sexual nature control a person's behavior. According to Freud, one's mind contains (sexual) memories, impulses, desires, feelings, etc., of which the individual is not conscious, but which influence his emotions and behavior. Thus Freud searched for sexual significances and told the patient what they meant. Page 9.

frog in even a pulp paper puddle, big: a variation of *better to be a big frog in a small pond than a little frog in a big pond,* meaning that one is better off being a person who is important in a limited area of activity rather than someone unimportant in a larger area. Page 20.

functional illiteracy: the condition whereby one's reading and writing abilities are not adequately developed, thus making it difficult or impossible to carry out the everyday activities that require these skills. Page 75.

G

Gambia, The: a state of western Africa that extends on both sides of the Gambia River, which flows into the Atlantic Ocean. Page 92.

"gangbanger": one who participates in a *gangbang,* an instance of violence involving members of a criminal gang. Page 96.

gauge: estimate or judge. Page 36.

gay: cheerful and happy. Page 32.

gee whiz: an exclamation of surprise or other strong feeling. Page 33.

geological: of, about or based on *geology,* the science that deals with the physical history of the Earth, the rocks of which it is composed, and the physical and chemical changes Earth has undergone or is undergoing. Page 52.

geometry, solid: a branch of geometry (the science that investigates the properties and relations of magnitudes in space) that particularly deals with solid, or three-dimensional, figures. Page 29.

George Washington University: a private university, founded in 1821, in the city of Washington, DC. Named after the first president of the United States, George Washington (1732–1799), it maintains various schools of education, including the School of Engineering and Applied Science and the Columbian College of Arts and Sciences. The university has a long history of supporting research in physics and other technical fields. Page 9.

gleeful: very happy or joyful. Hence *"a gleeful youth"* refers to a very happy or joyful period of one's life when one is young. Page 29.

glib: lacking understanding; shallow and superficial. Page 45.

glibly: in a way that lacks depth and substance; superficially. Page 4.

gorge: take in greedily, likened to swallowing large quantities of food. Page 22.

Governor's Office, California: the executive departments under the governor of California that oversee numerous agencies and programs operating at state level. Page 96.

grade average: also *grade point average,* the average of a student's grades over a fixed period, calculated by assigning a value of 4 to A, 3 to B, 2 to C, 1 to D and 0 to F. Page 78.

grade (first, second, third, fourth, etc.): the division of a school in the United States that is classified according to the progress or age of the pupils. For example, public schools are divided into twelve grades prior to college. Generally one starts first grade at the age of six, after kindergarten, and advances a grade each year until he has completed all twelve at the age of eighteen. Page 9.

gradient: a gradual approach to something, taken step by step, level by level, each step or level being, of itself, easily surmountable—so that finally, complicated and difficult activities can be achieved with relative ease. The term *gradient* also applies to each of the steps taken in such an approach. Page 43.

grammarian: one who is knowledgeable in grammar or in language generally, such as its structure, spelling, etc. Also, more generally, one who writes on the basic elements or principles of any science, art, discipline or practice; a person who studies and writes about grammar. Page 84.

grandly: in a grand (impressive, magnificent, etc.) manner. Page 13.

graphic: giving a clear and effective picture as if represented in a picture or drawing. Page 93.

grass-roots: characteristic of the common people, originally those especially of rural or nonurban areas, thought of as a fundamental political group and a source of independent popular opinion. Page 92.

gravel: small stones, often used to make the surface of paths and roads. Page 11.

gravitate: move gradually and steadily to or toward somebody or something as if drawn by some force or attraction. Page 29.

grieve: cause anxiety, trouble or sadness to somebody; burden. Page 29.

grim: harsh or uninviting in attitude and action. Page 3.

grip, lost (one's): failed to maintain an intellectual or mental hold of something. Page 75.

grisly: gruesomely unpleasant or creating a sense of horror. Page 20.

Guam: an island in the northwestern Pacific Ocean, a territory of the United States and site of US air and naval bases. Page 9.

gunnery: instruction in the operation and use of guns. Page 29.

GWU: an abbreviation for *George Washington University.* Page 19.

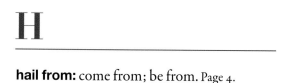

H

hail from: come from; be from. Page 4.

hallmark: any mark or special indication of genuineness, good quality, etc. Literally, a mark put on gold, silver and other fine metal objects that shows the quality of the metal and gives information about when and where the object was made. Page 96.

halls: large buildings or rooms for instruction, as at a college or university. Also, a corridor or passageway in such a building. *Hall* originally meant a castle or the large main room of the castle. Page 12.

Hammett, Dashiell: (1894–1961) highly influential American author of detective novels. Drawing on his years of work as a private detective, Hammett began writing in the early 1920s. With his realistic writing style, he created enduringly popular characters and plots, with a number of his best-known works, such as *The Maltese Falcon* (1930), later adapted for film. Page 14.

hands of, fell into the: came under the influence, power or control of. Page 87.

hang (someone) up: cause (someone) to become halted or suspended in progress. Page 51.

hard: showing little or no compassion or gentleness; severe. Page 20.

Harvard: the oldest university in the United States, located in Cambridge, Massachusetts. Founded in 1636, it provides instruction in a wide variety of subjects, including law, medicine, business, government, religion, arts and sciences. It is a center for research and education and has one of the largest and most comprehensive university libraries in the world. Page 15.

have-not: (of a person or nation) with little wealth or poor resources. Page 2.

havoc, play: create confusion or disorder in. Page 28.

headlong: happening quickly and suddenly. Page 9.

Heinlein, Robert: (1907–1988) American author considered one of the most important writers of science fiction. Emerging during science fiction's Golden Age (1939–1949), Heinlein went on to write many novels, including the classic *Stranger in a Strange Land* (1961). He won four Hugo Awards and was presented with the first Grand Master Nebula Award for lifetime achievement in science fiction. Page 14.

Helena: city and capital of Montana, a state in the northwestern United States bordering on Canada. Page 10.

helming: being at the head of, and directing, an organization. Page 97.

Henry, O.: pen name of William Sydney Porter (1862–1910), American short-story writer noted for his mastery of plot twists that build to an unexpected ending. Page 62.

herein: in this writing, document or the like. Page 4.

hi-fi: an abbreviation for *high fidelity*, extremely high-quality sound reproduction with minimal distortion that sounds as close to the original as possible. *Fidelity* (literally, faithfulness) is the degree to which a sound or picture reproduced or transmitted by any device resembles the original. Page 69.

hitherto: up to this time; until now. Page 57.

hive: a colony of honeybees. Page 14.

homonymic: of or characteristic of a *homonym,* a word that is spelled or pronounced in the same way as one or more other words but has a different meaning: *rowed* and *road* are homonyms. Page 62.

honorary: given or awarded for outstanding service or achievements, rather than for the completion of a required course of study. Page 24.

honors: official recognition of academic excellence and achievement. Page 4.

hub: a central point around which other things turn; a central point of activity, life, interest, etc. Page 91.

Hubbard Key to Life Course: a Scientology course that handles the reasons why a person cannot comprehend what he reads, writes and hears and why others cannot understand him. It results in a person who is in communication because he can express himself easily and clearly, both verbally and in writing, and can fully understand the communication he receives from others. The Key to Life Course is a major breakthrough in the field of communication. Page 4.

hue and cry: a public clamor, as of protest or demand. *Hu e cri,* a Middle English term, was an outcry that signified the pursuit of a criminal and alerted others, who were then legally obliged to give chase. Page 28.

hum with looms and lathes: be filled with the sounds of machinery. A *loom* is a machine for weaving cloth. A *lathe* is a machine for working wood or metal, in which the piece being worked is held and rotated while a cutting tool is applied to it. Page 21.

husbandry, animal: the science of breeding, feeding and tending domestic animals. Page 28.

hydraulic press: a device for applying pressure to flatten or shape something. *Hydraulic* means operated, moved or brought about by use of water or a fluid. Page 20.

I

ideological flow: the progress of ideas, as in laying out a logical series of statements, data, etc. Page 45.

ignoramuses: ignorant and stupid people. Page 2.

ill-: used in combination with another word, with the meaning of badly, wrongly or imperfectly. Page 16.

illegal professionals: a reference to American football, in which it is illegal for a professional player (one who receives money for playing) to play on a college football team, which is made up exclusively of amateurs (those who play for pleasure only). Page 12.

illicit: forbidden by law, rules or custom. Page 76.

impacts upon: has a strong effect on, especially in terms of blocking, modifying or producing such things as actions, changes, etc. Page 54.

impairment: the result or fact of being *impaired,* reduced or made less in value, excellence, etc. Page 75.

impediments: things that delay or stop the progress of something; obstacles. Page 36.

implicit: implied, rather than stated directly. Page 11.

imposingness: the state or quality of being *imposing,* making a strong impression because of great size, strength, dignity, etc.; impressive. Page 62.

impoverished: poor in resources in a certain field or area; deprived. Page 2.

inarticulate: lacking the ability to express oneself in clear and effective speech. Page 54.

inattentive: not paying attention. Page 68.

incentive: something that encourages or motivates somebody to do something. Page 13.

incidental(s): something that happens in connection with something else but is less important. Page 41.

incorrigible: that cannot be corrected or reformed, especially due to firmly established habits. Page 96.

inculcate: fix deeply into someone's mind by repeated statement; instruct persistently. Page 37.

individuation: a pulling back from; the action or process of becoming more and more separate and individual. Page 54.

infusion: the introduction or addition of some new quality or element to something. Page 3.

ingrained: (of a habit or attitude) firmly established. Page 75.

inner-city: in or of the usually older, poorer and more densely populated central section of a city, particularly when associated with social problems such as inadequate housing and high levels of crime and unemployment. Page 4.

innovative: new and original or taking a new and original approach. Page 82.

innumerable: very many or too many to be counted. Page 31.

insidious: operating or proceeding in an inconspicuous or seemingly harmless way but actually with grave effect; slowly and subtly harmful and destructive. Page 44.

insofar: to such a degree or extent. Page 27.

insomnia: inability to fall asleep or to remain asleep long enough to feel rested, especially as a problem continuing over time. Page 76.

institution, something of an: someone who, to a certain extent or degree, is well established in some customary relationship. Page 18.

integral: an essential or fundamental part of something. Page 45.

intent: something planned or the purpose that accompanies a plan. Page 5.

intermediate: coming between two points, stages or things. Page 57.

intriguing: arousing curiosity or interest. Page 13.

inveterate: settled or confirmed in a habit, practice or the like. Page 4.

ire: a feeling or display of deep anger or fury. Page 35.

irony: something that happens that is unsuitable or strange, not fitting with what might be expected to happen, especially when this seems absurd or laughable. Page 14.

itinerant: being in one place for a comparatively short time and then moving on to another place. Page 9.

J

Johnny read?, why can't: a reference to *Why Johnny Can't Read,* by Robert Flesch, a bestselling book from the mid-1950s that discussed problems in the teaching of reading and how to remedy them. Page 3.

junior high: a school attended after grade school and usually consisting of seventh grade through ninth grade. Page 46.

K

Kansas: a state in the western part of the central United States. Page 65.

killer bee: an aggressive honeybee that was accidentally bred in Brazil from types of bees native to Africa and Europe and which has spread north into Mexico and parts of the United States. Used figuratively. Page 14.

knucklebone: small objects used in fortunetelling, magic or the like, as when a witch doctor tosses knucklebones and observes their pattern to foretell future events or to answer questions regarding matters of health, etc. The belief is that the will of the gods is revealed through the pattern of the bones. Page 33.

L

labeling: assigning to a category, especially inaccurately. Page 3.

lackluster: without interest or excitement; dull. Page 33.

Lancelot: a knight in medieval legends of King Arthur's Round Table. Lancelot won fame for his bravery and was Arthur's favorite knight, but he had an affair with Queen Guinevere, Arthur's wife, and this led to his downfall. Page 32.

landmark: marking a significant change or turning point in something. From *landmark,* an event, idea or item that represents a significant or historic development. Page 96.

last word: the final decision on something. Page 67.

Latin: the language of ancient Rome and its empire. Latin was also used in Europe, especially during the Middle Ages (about the late 400s to the mid-1400s), as the language of government officials, doctors, lawyers, scholars and priests. Page 21.

latitude: an imaginary line joining points on the Earth's surface that are all of equal distance north or south of the equator. Page 16.

latterly: at a subsequent time; later. Page 5.

Learning Disability: a supposed condition describing someone as unable to learn basic skills. Page 4.

lectern: a stand with a slanted top, used to hold a book, speech, manuscript, etc., at the proper height for a reader or speaker. Page 15.

legacy: a situation that exists now because of events, actions, etc., that took place in the past. Page 84.

Leipzig school: the approach or method of "modern psychology" as formulated by German psychologist Wilhelm Wundt and others in 1879 in Leipzig, a city in eastern central Germany, the location of Leipzig University. Page 13.

letters: written artistic works in general; literature. Page 15.

leveler: something that tends to reduce or eliminate differences among people. Page 65.

life expectancy: the number of years that somebody can be expected to live, according to statistics. Page 93.

like as not: to a probable or likely extent. Page 35.

Lincoln, Abraham: (1809–1865) sixteenth president of the United States, who led the Northern states of the US to victory over the Southern states in the Civil War and abolished slavery. Page 62.

lines, through the: in or among the portions of the text of a poem. Page 32.

linguist: one who is skilled in the use of languages; one who speaks a language besides his own. Page 32.

linguistics: the study of languages and the nature and structure of speech, including the various sounds used in speaking, word formations, grammar, the structure of sentences and the derivations of words. Page 45.

lip service: an expression of agreement, support, etc., for something expressed in words only and not in deeds. In this context, *lip* means merely from the lips as opposed to from the heart or from a genuine commitment; *service* means conduct or performance that assists or benefits someone or something. Page 10.

listless: having or showing little or no interest in anything; not caring, apathetic. Page 101.

liturgy: a form and arrangement of public worship laid down by a church or religion. Page 84.

livingness: the quality, condition or fact of being alive or living. Page 64.

lo: used to direct attention to what is about to be said, meaning "look" or "see." Page 28.

locomotive(s): an engine that can move about by its own power on wheels, designed to push or pull a railroad train. Page 17.

long division: a method or instance of dividing one number by another number that has, usually, two or more digits, in which each step of the process is written out in full. Page 9.

looms and lathes, hum with: be filled with the sounds of machinery. A *loom* is a machine for weaving cloth. A *lathe* is a machine for working wood or metal, in which the piece being worked is held and rotated while a cutting tool is applied to it. Page 21.

loosest: not at all strict or exact. Hence *"educated in only the loosest sense of the word"* means the education was so poor it could only loosely (not exactly) be called education. Page 91.

Los Angeles basin: the region of the central part of the city of Los Angeles, California, and its southern suburbs, which lie in a *basin,* a low-lying area in the surface of the Earth. Bordered by the Pacific Ocean on the west and by hills and mountains on the other three sides, the Los Angeles basin is approximately 35 miles (56 kilometers) long and 15 miles (24 kilometers) wide. Page 93.

lost generation: individuals of about the same age who have had such limited opportunities that a successful future is very unlikely, therefore their lives are wasted (lost). Page 91.

Luzon: the largest island in the Philippines, situated in the northern part of the country. Page 29.

M

Maine: the northernmost state on the east coast of the United States. Page 65.

majesty: the impressive and attractive quality that something has, which causes admiration and respect for its beauty. Page 62.

major: a subject or field of study chosen by a student to represent his or her principal interest and upon which a large share of his or her efforts is concentrated. Page 12.

Malaysia: a country in Southeast Asia. It consists of two geographical regions divided by the South China Sea. Page 96.

malign: speak harmful untruths about; speak evil of. Page 29.

mallet: in polo, the long-handled stick or club used to hit the ball. Page 32.

manuscript: an author's work as written or typed, not a printed book. Page 26.

mark(s): a number or letter that is given to show the standard of someone's work or performance or is given to someone for answering something correctly. Page 21.

marred: spoiled something, making it poor or inadequate. Page 68.

marvel: 1. something that causes wonder, admiration or astonishment; a wonderful thing; a wonder. Page 57.

2. be filled with wonder or astonishment. Page 67.

mass: the actual physical objects, the things of life. Page 42.

mass education: education designed for and affecting large numbers of people. Page 14.

matriculated: enrolled in a college or university to get a degree, after having previously met entrance requirements, such as successfully passing an entrance examination. Page 12.

medieval: relating to or typical of the Middle Ages in Europe (from about the late 400s to the mid-1400s). Also, old-fashioned or outdated. Page 84.

melancholy: sadness and depression of spirits. Page 22.

"memory mind": a high degree of the mental ability of *remembering,* keeping or bringing back again facts previously learned, particularly through the mere use of memory without any understanding. Page 33.

Memphis: a river port on the Mississippi River in southwestern Tennessee (a state in the southeastern United States). Page 92.

messianic: done with or showing great enthusiasm, devotion and a crusading spirit suggestive of a *messiah,* a zealous leader of some cause or project. Page 12.

metaphysical: of or relating to *metaphysics,* the branch of philosophy concerned with the ultimate nature of existence or the nature of ultimate reality; that is above or goes beyond the laws of nature or is more than the physical. Page 18.

meter: rhythm in verse; measured, patterned arrangement of syllables, primarily according to stress or length. Page 32.

methodically: in a way that is careful, logical and orderly. Page 77.

middle (of the class): (of a member of a group or series) placed so as to have the same number of members on each side. Hence intermediate in rank, quality or ability. Page 35.

midterm: halfway through an academic *term,* each of the periods (usually three or four months in length) for instruction and study in a school. Page 10.

military-industrial complex: a network of a nation's military force together with all of the industries that support it. Page 17.

mining: digging into and searching through a rich source of supply for the purpose of obtaining items of use or value, likened to the process of removing minerals, precious stones or the like from the earth. Page 64.

minister: a person appointed to head an executive or administrative department of the government. Page 92.

ministry: any of the administrative governmental departments of certain countries, usually under the direction of a minister of state. Page 92.

misalignment: a state of being improperly coordinated or being out of agreement with, as in meaning or understanding. Page 54.

missing link: something that is absent from a sequence or series and is needed to connect its various parts and complete it. Page 81.

missionary: of or concerning the functions performed by those who are sent to another country by a church to spread its faith or to do social or medical work. Page 10.

Mississippi: the Mississippi River, the second-longest river in the United States (2,340 miles or 3,766 kilometers), which flows through the central states from the north down through the southern states to the Gulf of Mexico. Page 60.

Missouri: a state in the central United States. Page 91.

misunderstood word: a word that is *not* understood or is *wrongly* understood. Page 44.

mixing: the process of putting several soundtracks onto the two (or more) tracks of the final product. It is done through a mixing board. Page 68.

mocking: treating someone with ridicule or contempt. Page 65.

monosyllabic: having a vocabulary composed primarily of short, simple words or of words that have only one syllable. Page 54.

Montana: a state in the northwestern United States bordering on Canada, where L. Ron Hubbard lived as a young boy. Page 10.

moot: of little or no practical value or meaning; irrelevant; unimportant. Page 15.

moral: 1. of, pertaining to or concerned with the principles or rules of right conduct or the distinction between right and wrong. Page 1.
2. the conclusion or practical lesson contained in a story, an event or the like. Page 68.

Moretele: a community located north of Pretoria, the administrative capital of South Africa, which is in the northeastern part of the country. Page 92.

Morocco: a kingdom on the northwest coast of Africa, bordering the Mediterranean Sea on the north and the Atlantic Ocean on the west. Page 75.

Moss, Dr. Fred: (1893–1966) doctor, psychologist and chairman of the Department of Psychology at George Washington University from 1924 to 1936. Page 13.

mumbo jumbo: complicated and sometimes purposeless activity or language intended to obscure. Page 33.

N

NAACP: an abbreviation for *National Association for the Advancement of Colored People,* a civil rights organization in the United States. Founded in 1909, the NAACP works to ensure equality of rights for all people and an end to racial discrimination. Page 93.

National Institute for Literacy: a United States Government agency created in the early 1990s to develop methods of improving literacy for children and for adults. Page 94.

national socialism: the principles and practices of Adolf Hitler and the Nazis, such as the totalitarian principle of government, state control of all industry, forcible elimination of opposition, and racism, especially prejudice against Jewish people. Page 13.

Naval Academy: a college for training naval officers, located in Annapolis, Maryland (a state in the eastern part of the United States on the Atlantic Ocean). Page 29.

naval engineer: an engineer is one whose profession is concerned with the design, construction and use of engines, machines or structures, such as bridges, roads, canals, railways, harbors, drainage works, gas and waterworks, etc. Here the naval engineer is one working at a *naval shipyard,* a large enclosure adjoining the sea, in which naval ships are built, repaired and maintained. Page 11.

Nebraska: a state in the central part of the United States. Page 9.

New York Institute of Photography: a school of photography founded in New York City in 1910. It runs a correspondence course (where study materials are mailed to the students, who in turn mail their work back to the school for grading) that teaches the technology of photography with a view to training students to be top-level amateurs or paid professionals in the field. The course covers the fundamentals of the subject, both in theory and practical application, including styles of photography, lighting, darkroom techniques and so on. Page 41.

Nicaragua: the largest country in Central America, situated between the North Pacific Ocean and the Caribbean Sea. Page 20.

1984: a famous satirical novel by English author George Orwell (1903–1950), published in 1949. The novel is set in the future in a supposed "perfect society," but where freedom of thought and action have disappeared and the world is dominated by a few totalitarian states. The government maintains continual surveillance on its people, denying any privacy, with placards proclaiming "Big Brother [the all-powerful dictator of the state] Is Watching You." Page 60.

nipa hut: *nipa* is a palm tree of India and the Philippines, etc., whose leaves are used for thatching roofs, basketry, etc. A *nipa hut* is a small home that has a roof made from the leaves of a nipa palm. Page 11.

"no child left behind": a reference to the No Child Left Behind Act, an education-reform law passed in the United States in 2001 that sought to identify poorly performing schools through annual reading and math tests. The law called for corrective actions in persistently failing schools, including replacing certain teachers, revising the curriculum, etc., or risk being taken over by the state. Page 3.

nomenclature: a system or set of names or designations used in a particular field. Page 81.

'normous: a spelling that represents a child's pronunciation of *enormous,* very big in size. Page 31.

no-supper attitude: the attitude that a proper punishment for an offender is to be refused the evening meal. Page 56.

no-system: a condition in which there is lack of a *system,* an organized and coordinated method or procedure followed to accomplish a task or attain a goal. Page 67.

notion, took a: had an idea, opinion or belief. Page 32.

notwithstanding: in spite of; regardless of. Page 2.

nuance: a very slight difference in meaning, feeling, tone or the like. Page 59.

number-one: of a person, group, etc., that is first in rank, order, importance or the like. Page 28.

O

obtuse: hard to understand; so scholarly as to be unclear. Page 4.

offshoot: something that originated or developed from something else. Page 13.

oft: often (used in poetry and literature). Page 28.

ordered: having all elements in a neat, well-organized or regular arrangement. Page 13.

Oregon: a state in the northwest United States, on the Pacific coast. Page 96.

origination(s): a communication, something that a person volunteers. Page 57.

ornaments: decorative parts or additions, such as curved or flowing lines in written documents, that are not part of the writing, but that add grace or beauty. Page 67.

Orwell, George: pen name of Eric Arthur Blair (1903–1950), well-known English author who gained a reputation for his political shrewdness and his sharp satires. Writing both novels and essays, Orwell first achieved prominence in the 1940s for his two most well-known books, *Animal Farm* and *1984,* both of which reflect his lifelong distrust and disagreement with dictatorial government. Page 60.

ostensibly: outwardly appearing as such; as shown or put forth. Page 12.

outlander: somebody from another country or from a different region and thus a stranger. Page 65.

outline: a list of the main points of a subject to be written about. Page 22.

out of: not in, or no longer in, a given state or condition, as in *"out of communication."* Page 65.

overbearing: too confident and too determined to tell other people what to do, in a way that is unpleasant. Page 20.

overriding: most important. Page 4.

ox cart: a cart pulled by an *ox,* an adult of the cattle family. The ox has been used for centuries for pulling heavy loads, as on farms. Page 11.

Oxford: Oxford University, one of the oldest and best-known universities of the world, located in southern England. Page 29.

P

packing case: a large, strong box used for transportation or storage. Page 20.

pack, ran with the: carried out activities, such as hunting, with a group of (early) humans. *Pack* can be applied to a group of human beings when the group's behavior appears to be threatening or violent, like that of a group of animals that live and hunt together, especially wolves or dogs. Page 13.

pains, go to great: take great care or trouble to achieve a good result. Page 64.

panorama: a complete and comprehensive range. Page 44.

parallel: something that is very similar to another, sharing many characteristics. Page 13.

parlance: language; the style of speech or writing used in a particular context. Page 60.

parrot: repeat what someone else has said or written without understanding it or thinking about its meaning. Page 29.

passes for: is accepted as or believed to be. Often used with the implication of actually being something else. Page 84.

pastime: a way of spending time pleasantly; anything done for recreation, such as a hobby. Used humorously. Page 60.

pauper: a person who is without possessions or money. Hence someone without some (specified) item. Page 62.

Pavlov: Ivan Petrovich Pavlov (1849–1936), Russian physiologist, noted for his dog experiments. Pavlov presented food to a dog while he sounded a bell. After repeating this procedure several times, the dog (in anticipation) would salivate at the sound of the bell, whether or not food was presented. Pavlov concluded that all acquired habits, even the higher mental activity of Man, depended on conditioning. Page 13.

penal system: the organized group of courts, prisons, etc., that are concerned with punishment given by law. Page 1.

perennial(ly): lasting for a long time; enduring or continually recurring. Page 18.

perforce: by necessity; by force of circumstance. Page 41.

per se: by or in itself, essentially; without reference to anything else. Page 44.

perspective: a specific point of view in understanding or judging things or events, especially one that shows them in their true relations to one another. Page 26.

phonetic: having to do with *phonetics,* the study of speech sounds, their production and combination, and their representation by written symbols. Page 4.

physiological response: *physiological* means relating to the way living bodies function. *Response* means something done as a reaction to some influence, event, etc. *Physiological response* means outward physical signs or indications as a reaction (to something). Page 42.

pillar: something regarded as a fundamental or chief support, as of a field of study or activity, similar to a *pillar,* a strong column made of stone, metal or wood that supports part of a building. Page 9.

pitfall(s): a potential disaster or difficulty, often one that is unexpected or that cannot be anticipated. From the literal idea of a *pitfall,* a trap that is a deep hole in the ground disguised with leaves covering its top opening and having sides so steep that escape is impossible. Page 62.

pivotal: of vital or critical importance. Page 45.

plane: a level of existence, consciousness or development. Page 56.

plastic: a substance capable of being formed into various shapes and used, for example, by a makeup artist in modifying the features of an actor's face to allow him to play a specific role. Page 33.

plateau: level of attainment or achievement. Page 5.

plopped down: dropped or sat down quickly and heavily. Page 65.

plume of smoke: a rising column of smoke seen as comparable to a plume (feather). Page 21.

plummeting: decreasing rapidly in amount. Page 96.

polo: a game of Eastern (Indian) origin played on horseback by two teams of four players each who attempt to drive a small wooden ball through the opponents' goal with a mallet having a long, flexible handle. Page 32.

polysyllabic: consisting of several, especially four or more, syllables (words or parts of words pronounced with a single, uninterrupted sounding of the voice), such large words sometimes being employed by those who act very learned and serious. Page 60.

pompous: characterized by an exaggerated display of self-importance or dignity. Page 20.

ponies: literal translations of texts, used by students, often dishonestly, as an aid to studying a foreign language or during an examination. Page 32.

posing: assuming a certain attitude. Page 65.

postindustrial: of or relating to the time period after the industrial age. The *industrial age* refers to the widespread replacement of manual labor by machines, which began in Britain in the eighteenth century, with economies changing from agricultural to industrial and production of goods and the workforce moving from homes and small workshops to urban factories. The word *post* means after or later. Page 1.

potboilers: mediocre works of literature or art produced merely for financial gain. Page 75.

pour along: run or rush in great numbers or in rapid succession, as if sending a liquid or fluid along some channel. Page 65.

pragmatic: expressing opinions and views in an overbearing or intolerant way. Page 15.

praiseworthy: approved of and regarded as worthwhile. Page 64.

precedent(s): a previous instance or case that is, or may be, taken as an example or rule for subsequent cases or by which some similar act or circumstance may be supported or justified. Page 31.

precipitating: bringing about the occurrence of something, especially suddenly or rapidly. Page 2.

prefatory: of, pertaining to or of the nature of a *preface*, a preliminary statement in a book by an author or editor, setting forth its purpose and scope, etc. Page 86.

preposition: a word that shows the relationship between a person, place or thing and some other word (or words) in the sentence. For example, in "the book is *on* the table," the preposition *on* shows the relationship between the book and the table, indicating where the book is. Page 44.

prestige: estimation in the eyes of others; influence; reputation. Page 36.

primary school: a school that provides the first four to eight years of basic education. A *lower primary school* handles instruction for the youngest children in this group. Page 92.

prison-yard: of or having to do with a *prison yard,* the area of ground (a yard) within the walls of a *prison,* a secure place where somebody is confined as punishment for a crime or while waiting to stand trial. Page 3.

professionals, illegal: a reference to American football, in which it is illegal for a professional player (one who receives money for playing) to play on a college football team, which is made up exclusively of amateurs (those who play for pleasure only). Page 12.

Professor So-and-so: a made-up name. *So-and-so* is used when talking generally rather than giving a specific example of a particular person. Page 20.

programs: performances of recorded material, as voice, music or the like. Page 68.

proposition: a statement about something being considered or discussed. Page 14.

prose: ordinary written language, in contrast to poetry. Page 60.

province: the sphere or field of activity; the range of function. Page 54.

"provinces," the: the parts of a country outside of the capital or the largest cities, often regarded as lacking in correct speech, fashion, manners or taste. Page 64.

psychobabble: writing or talk influenced by the concepts and terminology of psychology or psychiatry and that contains inaccurate information and is deliberately confusing. Page 13.

psychostimulants: drugs that stimulate the central nervous system of the body. They are taken to supposedly increase attention span, but they are addictive and one has to take more of the drug to avoid experiencing depression and drowsiness. Page 42.

psychotropic(s): a drug that affects mental activity, behavior or perception; a mood-altering drug. Page 76.

public house: also called a *pub,* an establishment for the sale and consumption of beer and other drinks, often also serving food. Page 54.

public school: in England, an independent fee-charging secondary school, typically a single-sex boarding school. The public schools prepare students chiefly for the universities or for public service. Page 29.

Puebla State: a state in south central Mexico. Page 92.

pulp paper puddle, big frog in even a: a variation of better to be a *big frog in a small pond than a little frog in a big pond,* meaning that one is better off being a person who is important in a limited area of activity rather than someone unimportant in a larger area. Page 20.

pulpwood stock: relating to the rough type of paper (stock) used for printing inexpensive magazines, etc. The low-cost pulp used in its manufacture is made from wood fibers, which give a rough texture. Page 14.

purity: the quality or state of being *pure,* specifically, containing nothing that does not properly belong; free from alteration, error or foreign addition. Page 42.

Q

quality group articles: stories produced for the top-ranked pulp magazines, viewed as the "quality group" of magazines because they published the best writing by the most accomplished writers. Page 21.

quarter(s): a particular but unspecified person, group of people or area. Page 1.

R

rabid: extremely intense. Page 23.

radium: a white, highly radioactive metallic element. Page 23.

ramification(s): effects, consequences or results. Page 44.

rant: speak or shout in a loud, wild, extravagant way. Page 20.

ran with the pack: carried out activities, such as hunting, with a group of (early) humans. *Pack* can be applied to a group of human beings when the group's behavior appears to be threatening or violent, like that of a group of animals that live and hunt together, especially wolves or dogs. Page 13.

rapt: involved in, fascinated by or concentrating on something to the exclusion of everything else. Page 54.

rating: a classification or ranking as of people or things based on a review of their quality, standard or performance. Page 33.

rating, credit: a reference to the action of officially recognizing a person or organization as having met a standard or criterion. Page 29.

rationalized: worked out or logically concluded. Page 33.

"Reading Disorder 315": a made-up term for a supposed disorder that makes it difficult for a person to learn to read. Page 76.

reading-impaired: having lessened or nonexistent reading skills. Page 3.

reaffirming: continuing to point out something as true. Page 96.

recognition: the perception of something as existing or true; realization. Page 13.

recoil: (of an action) an unfavorable consequence for (the originator). Page 64.

reelingness: the state, quality or condition of having a sensation of *reeling,* feeling dizzy, unsteady or confused. The suffix *-ness* is used when forming nouns expressing a state, quality or condition. Page 43.

reform: a changing or altering of something viewed as wrong. Page 76.

reformation: improvement in form or quality; alteration to a better form; correction or removal of defects or errors. Page 84.

regimented: organized in a rigid system under strict discipline and control. Page 18.

regurgitate: repeat or reproduce what has been heard, read or taught, in a purely mechanical way, with no evidence of understanding. Page 78.

remedial: designed to help people with learning difficulties improve their skills or knowledge or relating to education designed to do this. From *remedy,* a means of setting something right or getting rid of something undesirable. Page 5.

renaissance: any revival or period of marked improvement and new life, in philosophy, art, literature, etc. Page 85.

repercussion: a widespread, indirect or unforeseen effect of an act, action or event. Page 101.

replete: well supplied (with something). Page 18.

repression: the condition that occurs when forceful control is used against such things as freedom of expression, thought, creativity or the like. Page 9.

reputed: widely believed. Page 62.

reshape: change the form or organization of something. Page 5.

resident: present in something. Page 37.

resides: is present in, exists or is inherent in something. Page 36.

resurgence: the act of rising again or springing again into being or vigor. Page 1.

resuscitate: make active or vigorous again. Page 93.

retiring: unwilling to be noticed or to be with other people. Page 70.

revelation: an action or instance of the showing or revealing of the truth about something. Page 17.

revere: feel deep respect or admiration for (someone or something). Page 23.

revolution: a sudden, complete or radical change of any kind in a condition, situation, subject, field of activity, etc. Page 5.

revolutionary: 1. of or relating to *revolution,* an overthrow or rejection and thorough replacement of an established system, social order or the like. Page 56.
2. completely new and different, especially in a way that leads to great improvements. Page 79.

rhetoric: the art of using words effectively, especially in writing. Page 18.

Rio: a shortened form of *Rio de Janeiro,* a seaport in southeast Brazil. Rio is the second-largest city in the country and one of the chief seaports of South America. Page 32.

rising star: the increasing fame or influence of an individual, seen as an indication that he or she will achieve great success. Page 18.

roan: a horse whose coat is a solid color, as reddish-brown, brown, black, etc., with a thick sprinkling of gray or white hairs. Page 75.

rod, rule of the: the use of a stick or cane for disciplining someone. Page 27.

roll book: a book in which a teacher keeps a record of the attendance or classwork of his pupils. Page 4.

rough and tumble: characterized by rough informality or disregard of usual rules; roughly vigorous. Page 60.

rub: an obstruction or difficulty that hinders, stops or alters the course of an argument, chain of thought or action. Page 13.

rubber meets the road, where the: a place or circumstance that is decisive or critical, the point at which something is put to an important test, shows real accomplishment or the like. Literally, the point where an automobile tire makes contact with the road surface. Page 94.

rubber stamp: authorization or approval given automatically or given by a person or institution whose power is formal but not real. Page 20.

S

Saint Hill: a manor (a large house and its land) located in East Grinstead, Sussex, in southern England. Saint Hill Manor was the residence of L. Ron Hubbard as well as the international communications and training center of Scientology from the late 1950s through the mid-1960s. Page 41.

saintly: fit for a *saint,* a particularly good or holy person. Page 12.

saith: an archaic form of the word *says.* Page 28.

salient: that stands out as important; particularly relevant. Page 4.

sanctified: made holy; sacred. Page 12.

San Pedro: a city in Southern California, annexed to Los Angeles. One of the world's largest man-made harbors, San Pedro is also the site of a United States military and naval base. Page 16.

saving grace: a redeeming quality or factor. Page 9.

scarcely: only to the slightest degree; hardly at all. Page 29.

scenario: an imagined sequence of possible events. Page 2.

scholarly: learned; with a great deal of knowledge, especially knowledge of an academic subject. Page 20.

scholarship: learning; knowledge acquired by study. Page 54.

scholastic: of or pertaining to schools, scholars or education; scholarly. Page 4.

Scholastic Aptitude Test: also known as the *Scholastic Assessment Tests,* examination required by most higher-education institutions in the United States for admission into college. The test is designed to assess math, verbal and reasoning abilities. Page 97.

Scientology: Scientology is the study and handling of the spirit in relationship to itself, universes and other life. The term Scientology is taken from the Latin *scio,* which means "knowing in the fullest sense of the word," and the Greek word *logos,* meaning "study of." In itself the word means literally "knowing how to know." Page 1.

scornfully: in a way that shows a great lack of respect for someone that one thinks is stupid, not good enough or the like. Page 28.

scrawled: written untidily or hastily, especially in large letters that are difficult to read. Page 15.

script: the letters or characters used in writing by hand; handwriting. Page 67.

Second World War: also *World War II* (1939–1945), conflict involving every major power in the world. On one side were the Allies (chiefly Great Britain, the US and the Soviet Union) and on the other side Axis powers (Germany, Japan and Italy). The conflict resulted from the rise of militaristic regimes in Germany, Japan and Italy after World War I (1914–1918). It ended with the surrender of Germany on May 8, 1945, and of Japan on August 14, 1945. Page 9.

self-advocating: having confidence in one's own abilities or character and presenting such self-assurance to others. Page 97.

semantics: the study or science of the meaning, or an interpretation of the meaning, of words, signs, sentences, etc. It comes from the Greek word *semantikos,* meaning significant. That is, words are symbols and are being given significance or meaning. Page 9.

semester: a division constituting half of the regular academic year, lasting typically from 15 to 18 weeks. Page 12.

sensorimotor: pertaining to the relationship between the senses and muscular movement; from *sensory,* relating to the senses, and *motor,* relating to muscular movement. *Sensorimotor development* is a term used by child psychologists in theorizing that there is a stage of learning in which a child uses his senses to find out about his body and objects in the environment. Page 13.

sentiment: a thought or an attitude based on feeling or emotion. Page 18.

sergeant(s): a subordinate (lower-ranking) officer, often in charge of training the troops. Page 35.

Shakespeare: William Shakespeare (1564–1616), English poet and dramatist; the most widely known author in all English literature. Page 18.

Shandong: a coastal province of northeast China. Page 4.

shirked: avoided or neglected something, such as assignments, work, a duty or responsibility. Page 21.

shroud: something that covers or conceals like a garment. Page 22.

sideline: an activity that is additional to the main thing one does. Page 41.

singular: of unusual quality; uncommon; unique. Page 18.

singularly: in a way that is concerned with one separate person or thing. Page 1.

sister: denoting an organization that has a relationship to another of common origin, shared interests, similar problems or the like. Page 96.

slide rule: a ruler with a sliding central strip, marked with graduated scales, in use since the mid-1600s for making precise, rapid calculations, especially for multiplication and division. Page 28.

small craft: a vessel that is of relatively small size. Page 16.

smug(ly): contentedly confident of one's abilities, accomplishments and the like. Page 20.

snarled: thrown into a state of confusion; tangled up. Page 9.

social advancement: the promotion of a person so that he assumes a higher rank or status in society. Page 84.

social standing: one's position, reputation or status in society. Page 84.

soften: become less sharply noticeable or distinct. Page 65.

solemnity: a serious or dignified feeling, character or appearance. Page 20.

solid geometry: a branch of geometry (the science that investigates the properties and relations of magnitudes in space) that particularly deals with solid, or three-dimensional, figures. Page 29.

solitude: a place, situation or the like of being alone without other people. Page 28.

something of an institution: someone who, to a certain extent or degree, is well established in some customary relationship. Page 18.

South Pacific: the region of the Pacific Ocean lying south of the equator, including its islands. It extends southward from the equator to Antarctica. Page 11.

South Sea Islands: the islands of the South Pacific Ocean. Page 65.

Spanish Lake: the international headquarters and training campus of Applied Scholastics International, in Spanish Lake, a community located near St. Louis in the eastern part of Missouri, a state in the central United States. Page 88.

spawned: brought forth; produced. Page 3.

spearhead: a group, person or the like that acts as the leading or driving element or force in an undertaking. Literally, a *spearhead* is the sharp pointed head that forms the piercing end of a spear. Page 56.

spearheading: of or characteristic of something that *spearheads,* acts as the leading or driving element or force in an undertaking. *See also* **spearhead.** Page 91.

specimen: an example of something, regarded as typical of its class or group. Page 67.

specter: literally, a *specter* is a ghost, especially one that causes fear or dread. Hence a specter is something that haunts, instills fear or disturbs the mind, thus the idea of something unpleasant that might happen in the future. Page 3.

spurred: encouraged (a person or organization) to take action or make greater efforts in achieving something. Page 22.

squads right: a command used in marching to get the squads (smallest military unit) to change direction to the right. Page 22.

stalks: moves silently and threateningly through (a place). Page 14.

stance: an attitude or view taken about something. Page 84.

standing, social: one's position, reputation or status in society. Page 84.

stands affirmation: acts as a demonstration or evidence of the truth of a statement. Page 97.

starched collar: the collar of a man's shirt to which has been applied *starch,* a substance used to stiffen textile fabrics before ironing. Page 20.

star, rising: the increasing fame or influence of an individual, seen as an indication that he or she will achieve great success. Page 18.

stately: having a dignified manner. Page 20.

stature: importance or reputation gained by ability or achievement. Page 36.

steamer: a large vessel propelled by one or more steam engines. Page 21.

stern: hard, harsh or severe in manner or character. Page 84.

stirring: exciting or thrilling. Page 32.

stock in trade: any resource, practice or device characteristically employed by a given person or group. Page 84.

stooped: with the head and shoulders bent forward and downward. Page 18.

St. Petersburg: a city in western Florida (a southeastern state in the United States), near Tampa. Page 24.

straight A's, tips for: pieces of practical advice on how to get the best marks (A's) consistently (straight). Page 47.

strains: figuratively, becomes stretched or forced beyond the normal or customary limits. Page 24.

Study Technology: the term given to the methods developed by L. Ron Hubbard that enable individuals to study effectively. It is an exact technology that anyone can use to learn a subject or to acquire a new skill. It provides an understanding of the fundamental principles of how to learn and gives precise ways to overcome the barriers and pitfalls one can encounter during study, such as going by misunderstood words or symbols. Page 4.

stultified: made worthless or useless. Page 5.

stultify: cause somebody or something to seem unintelligent or silly. Page 77.

stumbling block: something that stands in the way of achieving a goal or of understanding something; an obstacle. Page 32.

style: a method or custom of acting or performing; a distinctive and particular method or manner of doing something or expressing oneself, such as a way of writing, speaking or painting. Page 15.

subordinate: make subservient (of lesser importance); place in a position dependent upon or under the domination of. Page 13.

sub-Sahara: situated or originating in regions of the African continent south of the *Sahara,* the world's largest desert, which covers much of northern Africa. Page 92.

subtleties: careful distinctions that show refined analysis, perception or understanding and that convey exact meanings. Page 85.

suffice (it) to say: used to indicate that one is presenting something in a brief way, without necessarily giving all the details. Page 15.

suite(s): a group of rooms designed to be used together. Page 47.

sullen: showing silent resentment. Page 14.

sultry: oppressively hot and damp. Page 10.

summate: add together; sum up. Page 28.

sum of his evolutionary parts: a total of separate things that have come about because of *evolution,* a very ancient theory that all plants and animals developed from simpler forms and were shaped by their surroundings rather than being planned or created. Page 13.

sums: arithmetical problems to be solved or such problems worked out and having the various steps shown, as done in school. Page 10.

sunburst: a sudden appearance of someone or something thought of as bringing hope, happiness or the like, similar to the sudden appearance of the Sun from behind clouds. Page 22.

superintend: be responsible for and supervise (something)—for example, a project or job. Page 29.

superintendent: a person who oversees or directs some work, enterprise, establishment, organization, district, etc.; supervisor. Page 31.

suppress: prevent something from happening, operating or becoming apparent, or restrain something and limit its effects. Page 55.

surly: unfriendly, bad-tempered and often rude. Page 3.

surmise: conclude or suppose that something is the case. Page 44.

surveyor: somebody whose occupation is taking accurate measurements of land areas to determine boundaries, elevations and dimensions. Page 35.

Sussex: a former county of southeastern England, now divided into two counties, East Sussex and West Sussex. Saint Hill is located in East Grinstead, West Sussex. Page 41.

switch, thrown the wrong: literally, changed a connection on or redirected a railroad track by moving a lever connected to a *switch,* a track structure on a railroad for diverting moving trains from one track to another, commonly consisting of a pair of movable rails. Throwing the wrong switch would send a train onto the wrong rails, causing it to derail (go off the rails). Used figuratively. Page 17.

symbolic: involving the use of symbols. Page 13.

symbolized: represented in the manner of a *symbol,* a written or printed sign or character that represents something in a particular context. Page 45.

synonym(s): a word meaning the same, or almost the same, as another word in the same language. Page 52.

T

tabulator: literally, a business machine for tabulating data, especially one that sorts and selects information from a series of marked or perforated cards fed into it. Used figuratively in reference to the capabilities of the mind. Page 33.

taciturn: habitually uncommunicative or reserved in speech and manner. Page 3.

Tacoma: a seaport on the west coast of the United States, in the state of Washington. Page 9.

take the flame out: do away with angry words (as in an argument). Figuratively, *flame* is an intense emotion, such as anger or passion, likened to the flames of a fire. Page 59.

Tale of Two Cities: a historical novel by the English author Charles Dickens. The story focuses on events in London and Paris in the late 1700s during the French Revolution. Page 33.

talking down to: speaking to a person as if he were less intelligent, as by using obviously simple words. Page 57.

technology: the methods of application of an art or science as opposed to mere knowledge of the science or art itself. In Scientology, the term *technology* refers to the methods of application of Scientology principles to improve the functions of the mind and rehabilitate the potentials of the spirit, developed by L. Ron Hubbard. Page 1.

teeth, armed to the: fully equipped with what is considered needful. *To the teeth* means lacking nothing, completely. Figuratively, someone who looks *armed to the teeth* would be someone who looks fully prepared to accomplish something. Page 76.

telltale: serving to reveal or disclose something that is not intended to be known. Page 75.

Tempest, The: a tragicomedy (a dramatic or other literary composition combining elements of both tragedy and comedy) by William Shakespeare. *The Tempest* is about a storm, a shipwreck and the adventures of those who were shipwrecked on an enchanted island. Page 18.

Tennyson: (1809–1892) Alfred, Lord Tennyson, English poet noted for his skills in composing a wide variety of poetry and a remarkable ability to present fine shades of meaning in his works. Page 32.

term, at the: at the conclusion of the *term,* one of the two periods in the year during which instruction is given in a school, college, etc. Page 19.

thatched: having a roof made of *thatch,* a plant material such as palm leaves, straw or the like. Page 10.

theme: a short essay or written exercise for a student. Page 18.

therefrom: from that thing; from that. Page 3.

thick: (of an accent) readily noticeable or distinct. Page 65.

third-world: of or relating to the underdeveloped nations of the world, especially those with widespread poverty. Page 2.

Thompson, S. P.: Silvanus Phillips Thompson (1851–1916), British physicist, lecturer and writer on a wide range of technical and scientific subjects. His *Calculus Made Easy* (1910) has remained one of the most popular basic texts on calculus ever written. Page 29.

Thorndike: Edward Lee Thorndike (1874–1949), American psychologist and educator who stressed that Man is an animal governed by stimulus-response behavior. Thorndike influenced teachers to incorporate such views in their teaching of children. Page 12.

tide: the moving force of civilization, likened to a current or a body of flowing water. Page 64.

time clock: a clock with an attachment that may be activated to punch or stamp or record the exact time on a card or tape, used to keep a record of the time of something, as of the arrival and departure of employees. Page 22.

tips for straight A's: pieces of practical advice on how to get the best marks (A's) consistently (straight). Page 47.

tom-tom beating: a *tom-tom* is a drum of Native American origin, commonly played with the hands and used widely in ceremonies and rituals. The phrase *beating the tom-tom* is a variation of *beating the drum,* vigorously promoting, supporting or loudly publicizing (something). Likened to the beating of a drum for ceremonial, promotional or other purposes. Page 33.

topic sentence(s): a sentence that states the main or central thought of a paragraph or of a larger unit of writing and is usually placed at or near the beginning. Page 22.

touted: praised or recommended, often in a persistent manner. Page 4.

township: (in South Africa) a segregated residential settlement for blacks, located outside a city or town. Page 91.

transcultural: across, as in from one culture to another. By *culture* is meant the ideas, customs, skills, arts, etc., of a people or group, that are transferred, communicated or passed along to following generations. Page 3.

Transkei: in South Africa, a former *homeland,* a partially self-governing region created and set aside for the black population under the former policy of apartheid. Since the end of apartheid, Transkei has been part of *Eastern Cape Province,* a province in southeastern South Africa, on the Indian Ocean. Page 92.

translate: change something into (another form, condition or the like). Page 45.

trappings: the outward signs, features or objects associated with a particular situation, role or thing. Page 84.

treatise: a formal, usually extensive, written work on a subject. Page 21.

trick question: a question designed to elicit more information than it appears to on the surface. Page 13.

turns, by: in succession; consecutively. Page 5.

turn (something): move a knob, button or switch so as to change or stop the operation of a device, machine or the like. Page 69.

tutorial: characteristic of a lesson or a teaching session spent individually or in a small group under the direction of one teacher. Page 96.

Twentieth Century Limited: an express steam train that mainly ran between New York City and Chicago from 1902 to 1967. The *Twentieth Century Limited* was pulled by the world's first streamlined, high-powered steam engine and could make the trip between New York City and Chicago in eighteen hours. Page 17.

U

unashamedly: in a way that is not ashamed or embarrassed and not feeling the need to apologize to others. Page 41.

uncorrelated: not having established the proper relation between. Page 28.

unction: real or pretended earnestness or fervor, apparently arising from deep emotion and often expressed in solemn language. Page 28.

underscore: emphasize something, likened to marking with a score (line drawn or scratched) underneath the printed words on a page. Page 54.

UNESCO: United Nations Educational, Scientific and Cultural Organization, an agency of the United Nations established in 1946 to encourage nations to work together in the areas of education, science, culture and communication. Through such cooperative endeavors, UNESCO hopes to encourage universal respect for justice, laws, human rights and fundamental freedoms. Page 3.

University of California: a state-supported educational institution founded in the 1800s and located in California, with nine separate campuses in locations throughout the state, including Los Angeles. Page 78.

unswerving: not changing or becoming weaker. Page 33.

upheaval: a strong or sudden change in political, social or living conditions. Page 2.

utterance: something expressed, such as a word or words, whether written or spoken. Also, the action or manner of speaking. Page 60.

V

vehicle: a medium of communication, expression or display. Page 4.

Venezuela: a country in northeastern South America. Page 92.

veritable: possessing all of the distinctive qualities of the person or thing specified. Page 12.

Virginia: a state in the eastern United States, south of Washington, DC. Page 97.

Voltaire: assumed name of François Marie Arouet (1694–1778), French dramatist, philosopher and poet. Voltaire believed in freedom of thought and respect for all men and he spoke out against intolerance, tyranny and superstition. As part of his philosophy, he maintained that men can agree about two or three points that they can understand, but they can only argue to no purpose about two or three thousand that they can never understand. Page 59.

volume meter: a meter used with sound-reproducing or recording equipment that measures the average sound levels (loudness or softness) of a program. Page 69.

vulgar, the: ordinary people regarded or spoken of as a group. Page 84.

W

wares: articles offered for sale. Page 21.

"warrior": somebody who fights, especially a member of a street gang. Page 93.

washed-out: exhausted or lacking vitality and strength. Page 44.

wayside, by the: figuratively, as an additional activity that happens alongside the main activity. From the literal meaning of *wayside,* the edge of a road. Page 33.

wear: clothing typically worn for a particular purpose or of a particular type. Page 3.

wellspring: a plentiful source or supply of something, from the literal meaning, a source of a spring or stream. Page 88.

were, as it: if one might so put it; a phrase used to indicate that a word or statement is perhaps not formally exact though practically right. Page 14.

whence: from what source, origin or cause. Page 14.

whereupon: at which time or as a result of. Page 3.

wherewithal: that with which to do something; means or resources for the purpose or need. Page 80.

whole cloth: all at once or all in one piece. In the fifteenth century, whole cloth referred to a piece of cloth that ran the whole length of a loom (an apparatus used for weaving fabrics). An item made of such was considered superior to one made of different pieces of cloth sewn together. Page 9.

wholeheartedly: in a way that is *wholehearted,* characterized by enthusiasm, passion or commitment. Page 4.

Wilbur, William Allen: (1864–1945) a professor of English at George Washington University in the late 1800s and dean of one of the GWU colleges in the early 1900s. Page 18.

wings, in the: ready to appear or begin doing something; (for the moment) taking no part in the action. From the theatrical expression *waiting in the wings,* standing to the right or left of the stage, out of sight of the audience, ready to make an entrance. Page 2.

wit, to: used to introduce a list or explanation of what one has just mentioned. Originally a phrase used in law, *that is to wit,* which meant that is to know, that is to say. Page 2.

Woolworth Building: a sixty-story building in New York City, New York, built in 1913. It was the world's largest office building when built. It held that position for nearly twenty years. Page 11.

word association: a psychoanalytic method developed by Sigmund Freud for diagnosing what was wrong with a person. *Association* means an idea, image, etc., unconsciously suggested by or connected with something other than itself. In word association, the practitioner got an idea of what was wrong with the person by observation and then asked the person what came to mind instantly when a particular word (one which seemed to the practitioner to have something to do with what was wrong with the person) is spoken. The practitioner would use that to try to figure out what was upsetting the person. Page 10.

word chain: when one or more misunderstood words appear within the definition of the word the student is already clearing, this is called a *word chain*. Page 52.

Word Clearing: the subject and action of clearing away the ignorance, misunderstoods and false definitions of words and the barriers to their use. *Clearing* in this sense means making free of confusion, doubt or uncertainty. Page 45.

word one: the very first word (of something written). Page 3.

worldliness: the quality or an instance of being *worldly*, experienced in and knowledgeable about human society and its ways. Page 22.

World War I: (1914–1918) the war fought between the Allies (Britain, France, Russia and also the United States after 1917) and the Central Powers (Germany, Austria and other European countries). The war ended when Germany was defeated in 1918. Page 56.

World War II: also *Second World War* (1939–1945), conflict involving every major power in the world. On one side were the Allies (chiefly Great Britain, the US and the Soviet Union) and on the other side Axis powers (Germany, Japan and Italy). The conflict resulted from the rise of militaristic regimes in Germany, Japan and Italy after World War I (1914–1918). It ended with the surrender of Germany on May 8, 1945, and of Japan on August 14, 1945. Page 60.

wrought: brought about or caused. Page 76.

Wundt: Wilhelm Wundt (1832–1920), German psychologist and physiologist; the originator of modern psychology and the false doctrine that Man is no more than an animal. Page 13.

Y

YMCA: abbreviation for *Young Men's Christian Association*, an international community-service organization that encourages constructive social, physical and educational activities for youths and adults of both sexes. The association adheres to Christian principles but imposes no religious qualifications on its members. Page 29.

yoke: something regarded as oppressive or burdensome. Literally, a *yoke* is a frame fitting over the neck and shoulders of a person, used for carrying pails or baskets. Page 87.

Z

"zero-zero world": a world (all that belongs to a particular sphere of activity) characterized as being made up of people or things that are worthless or insignificant. Page 12.

zest: great enthusiasm, liveliness or energy. Page 33.

Zimbabwe: a country in Southern Africa, formerly known as Southern Rhodesia and then as Rhodesia. Zimbabwe was named after the famous fourteenth-century stone-built city of Great Zimbabwe, located in the country's southeast. Page 92.

zoology: the scientific study of animals, especially with regard to their structure and behavior. Page 29.

INDEX

THE
L. RON HUBBARD
SERIES

"To really know life," L. Ron Hubbard wrote, "you've got to be part of life. You must get down and look, you must get into the nooks and crannies of existence. You have to rub elbows with all kinds and types of men before you can finally establish what he is."

Through his long and extraordinary journey to the founding of Dianetics and Scientology, Ron did just that. From his adventurous youth in a rough and tumble American West to his far-flung trek across a still mysterious Asia; from his two-decade search for the very essence of life to the triumph of Dianetics and Scientology—such are the stories recounted in the L. Ron Hubbard Biographical Publications.

Drawn from his own archival collection, this is Ron's life as he himself saw it. With each volume of the series focusing upon a separate field of endeavor, here are the compelling facts, figures, anecdotes and photographs from a life like no other.

Indeed, here is the life of a man who lived at least twenty lives in the space of one.

For Further Information Visit
www.lronhubbard.org

The L. Ron Hubbard Series
A PROFILE

To order copies of *The L. Ron Hubbard Series*
or L. Ron Hubbard's Dianetics and
Scientology books and lectures, contact:

US AND INTERNATIONAL

BRIDGE PUBLICATIONS, INC.
5600 E. Olympic Blvd.
Commerce, California 90022 USA
www.bridgepub.com
Tel: (323) 888-6200
Toll-free: 1-800-722-1733

UNITED KINGDOM AND EUROPE

NEW ERA PUBLICATIONS
INTERNATIONAL ApS
Smedeland 20
2600 Glostrup, Denmark
www.newerapublications.com
Tel: (45) 33 73 66 66
Toll-free: 00-800-808-8-8008